MW01062328

# WILL IT FREEZE?

# WILL IT FREEZE ?

Compiled for Home & Freezer Digest
by Joan Hood
with additional research by Vivian Donald

**CHARLES SCRIBNER'S SONS**

**NEW YORK**

Copyright © British European Associated Publishers
Ltd. *(Home & Freezer Digest)*, 1976, 1980.
First published by Charles Scribner's Sons 1982.

**Library of Congress Cataloging in Publication Data**

Hood, Joan.
  Will it freeze?

  1. Food, Frozen. 2. Home freezers. I. Donald,
Vivian. II. Home & freezer digest. III. Title.
TX610.H66 1982      641.4'53      81-21484
ISBN 0-684-17495-2                    AACR2

1 3 5 7 9 11 13 15 17 19     F/C     20 18 16 14 12 10 8 6 4 2


Printed in the United States of America.

# Contents

# Introduction

Will it freeze? How often have you asked yourself that question, when wondering whether to take advantage of a bargain buy, when faced with a glut crop from your own or a friend's garden, or when you have an unexpected quantity of left-overs which you are unable to use up quickly?

The first part of this book provides the answer and also suggests how you can save time by preparing extra amounts of sauces, casseroles, cakes, desserts etc. when you are cooking one meal, and freezing the surplus to use on another occasion when time is short. The Dictionary of Foods also gives advice on the best way to freeze different foods, on their storage time and on how to use them, whether after thawing or from frozen. It advises against freezing some foods which deteriorate when frozen or which are as quick to prepare from scratch as to use from the freezer. Dry goods which are obviously best kept in the kitchen cabinet – flour, sugar, corn flakes, for example – are not listed.

If you want to freeze a made-up dish, look up its individual ingredients in the Dictionary and you will be able to gauge how successfully and for how long the dish will freeze by the ingredient with the shortest freezer life.

The Dictionary of Freezer Terms, the second part of this handbook, explains words that prospective freezer buyers and freezer owners will come across. It covers terms referring to the freezer, its functioning and position, to the insurance policies relating to freezers, to methods of freezing foods and to equipment you will need to make the best use of your freezer.

The third section, Freezer Management, contains chapters of useful background information and advice on using your freezer and on preparing foods before and after they have been in the freezer.

# DICTIONARY
# OF
# FOODS

## Almonds

These can be frozen whole, chopped, flaked or toasted. Do not salt. Wrap in foil in convenient quantities, making sure to exclude air from the package.

RECOMMENDED FREEZER LIFE: plain, 1 year; toasted, 4 months.

TO USE: thaw for 3 hours at room temperature.

## Anchovies

Because canned anchovies are so salty and salt tends to oxidise and lead to rancidity, they should not be frozen. If you open a can of anchovies and have some left over tip them, with their oil, into a small jar and cover with a lid or piece of foil. Store in a cool place. The oil acts as a preservative.

## Apples

Choose firm, ripe apples with a good flavour and freeze them in any of the following ways.

*Sliced:* peel, core and cut apples into ½-in (1-cm) slices and because they discolour quickly when exposed to the air, drop them into a bowl of cold water to which you have added salt - ½oz (15g) salt to 2 pts (1 l) of water. Rinse just before blanching - about ½lb (250g) at a time - in boiling water for 1 minute. Cool under the cold tap, drain and dry gently on kitchen paper. For free-flow packs spread apple slices on trays, freeze and then tip into a polythene bag. Frozen this way you can just pour out the required quantity and use from frozen. If you prefer, pack them in sugar or plain syrup.

*Dry sugar pack:* mix apple slices with sugar - 1 lb (500g) sugar to 4 lb (2 kg) fruit - and pack in polythene bags or rigid containers.

*Plain syrup pack:* make a medium syrup by dissolving 10oz (300g) sugar in 1pt (600ml) boiling water. Leave until cold before using. Pack fruit into rigid containers, cover with syrup leaving ½-1in (1-2cm) headspace for expansion. To keep the fruit well covered by the syrup and avoid discolouring, put crumpled greaseproof or freezer paper on top of syrup then leave ½-1in (1-2cm) headspace above the paper. Thaw overnight in fridge or 4 hours at room temperature.

*Purée:* wash and slice the apples. Do not core or peel. Put into a pan with just enough water to prevent the apples sticking and cook to a pulp. If you sieve or liquidise the apples in the blender, peel and core before cooking, add a little lemon juice and sweeten to taste. Cool and pack into rigid containers leaving ½-1in (1-2cm) headspace. Pack in small quantities, enough to suit your family's needs. Use from frozen for apple sauce, thaw overnight in fridge or 3 hours at room temperature for fools and soufflés.

*Baked:* use large good quality apples. Wash well and core. Fill centre with butter and sugar or raisins or mincemeat or brown sugar. Place in dish with a little water and bake (400°F, 200°C) until tender but still firm, about ¾-1 hour. When cold, freeze unpacked. Then pack in a rigid container with a sheet of moisture- and vapour-proof paper between apples. You can then remove the number you require without disturbing the rest. Heat through from frozen (375°F, 190°C) for 20 minutes.

See *Ascorbic Acid* for how to freeze fruit without sugar.

RECOMMENDED FREEZER LIFE: apple slices, 1 year; dry sugar pack, syrup pack and purée, 6 months; baked apples, 3 months.

## Apple Juice

This is a good way of using windfalls. Wash the fruit, remove any bruised or damaged parts and cut into thick slices without peeling or coring. Put into a pan with water to about a quarter of the depth of the fruit. Simmer until the apples are reduced to a pulp, then strain through a jelly bag

or muslin. When the juice is completely cold pour into rigid containers leaving ½-1 in (1-2 cm) headspace, or use ice cube trays and store the resultant frozen blocks in polythene bags.
RECOMMENDED FREEZER LIFE: 9 months.

## Apricots

Fresh apricots can be frozen in sugar or syrup or as a purée. Wash the fruit, cut in half and stone but do not peel. Drop the halves into a solution of water and lemon juice, using 3 tbs lemon juice to 2 pts (1 l) of water. This prevents them discolouring.

*Dry sugar pack:* drain and pack in dry sugar using 4 oz (125 g) sugar to each 1 lb (500 g) fruit. To use, thaw overnight in fridge or 2 hours at room temperature.

*Cold syrup:* pack prepared fruit into rigid containers and cover with cold syrup made by dissolving 8 oz (250 g) sugar in 1 pt (600 ml) boiling water. Put a piece of crumpled greaseproof or freezer paper over the top of the fruit to keep it below the syrup and leave ½-1 in (1-2 cm) headspace. Thaw overnight in fridge or 3 hours at room temperature.

*Cooked in syrup:* fruit that is not quite ripe is best cooked before freezing. Wash, halve and stone the apricots and put immediately into a saucepan of syrup made in the proportion of 8 oz (250 g) sugar to 1 pt (600 ml) water. Cook gently until the fruit is soft but still retains its shape. Allow fruit and syrup to become cold. Pour gently into rigid containers leaving ½-1 in (1-2 cm) headspace and freeze. Thaw overnight in fridge or 3 hours at room temperature.

*Purée:* it is best to freeze very ripe fruit as purée. Cook with just enough water to prevent the fruit sticking. Sieve, sweeten to taste - about 4 oz (125 g) sugar to 1 lb (500 g) fruit - and pack in rigid containers, leaving ½-1 in (1-2 cm) headspace. Thaw overnight in fridge or 3 hours at room temperature.

See *Ascorbic Acid,* for how to freeze fruit without sugar.

RECOMMENDED FREEZER LIFE: dry sugar packs, cold, and cooked in syrup, 1 year; purée, 4 months.

13

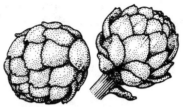

## Artichokes, Globe

Take off outer leaves, wash, trim stems. Have ready a large saucepan of boiling water and blanch up to six at a time for 7 minutes. Start timing when the water comes back to the boil. Plunge the artichokes immediately into iced or running cold water. When cool, drain, package and freeze.

RECOMMENDED FREEZER LIFE: 1 year.

TO USE: thaw overnight in fridge or 4 hours at room temperature.

## Artichokes, Jerusalem

These can be left in the ground all winter and dug as required so it is not worth taking up freezer space with them except in puréed form. They make a delicate and delicious soup in minutes if you have the purée already in your freezer. Scrub and peel the artichokes. Cut up roughly and put in a heavy saucepan with butter - 1 oz (30 g) to 1 lb (500 g) artichokes. Over a gentle heat turn the artichokes over and over to coat them in the melting butter. Add ¾ pt (450 ml) of chicken stock, season and simmer until tender. Sieve or liquidise in the blender. Cool and pack in rigid containers leaving ½-1 in (1-2 cm) headspace.

RECOMMENDED FREEZER LIFE: 3 months.

TO USE: put frozen purée into saucepan and heat gently. Stir in a little over ½ pt (300 ml) milk, simmer, adjust seasoning and serve hot garnished with croûtons.

14

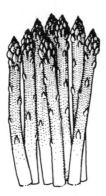

## Asparagus

This is a luxury vegetable with a short season. For perfection, it should be absolutely fresh, so only freeze it if you have a glut of it in the garden. Cut off the woody ends of the stalks. Wash, scrape and trim into even lengths. Grade into thick and thin stems. Don't tie into bundles. Blanch in boiling water: 4 minutes for thick stems and 2 minutes for thin stems. Cool and drain well. Pack carefully into rigid containers.

RECOMMENDED FREEZER LIFE: 1 year.

TO USE: thaw overnight in fridge or 4 hours at room temperature.

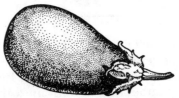

## Aubergines/ Eggplant

Choose firm eggplants with dark, glossy skins. Wash them and cut into ½in (1-cm) slices. Blanch for 4 mins. Drain, cool, and pat dry on absorbent paper and open-freeze. To do this spread eggplant slices on baking sheets and freeze uncovered. Then tip the slices into a polythene bag and seal. When required, tip out what you need, re-seal the bag and return it to the freezer.

To avoid discolouration blanch them as soon as possible after slicing.

15

If you want to freeze eggplants as part of a made-up dish like moussaka, slice them into a colander, salt lightly and leave for about ½ hour. Rinse thoroughly and dry them and they are ready for frying. The salting and draining rids them of any bitterness and excess moisture.

RECOMMENDED FREEZER LIFE: 1 year.

TO USE: cook slices from frozen or thaw overnight in fridge or 4 hours at room temperature.

**Avocado Pears**

These are best frozen as a purée which can be used later for soups or dips. Peel the fruit, remove the stone and purée the pulp adding 3 tbs lemon juice to 2 pts (1 l) purée. Pack in rigid containers leaving ½-1 in (1-2 cm) headspace for expansion.

RECOMMENDED FREEZER LIFE: 2 months.

TO USE: thaw overnight in fridge or 4 hours at room temperature.

**Baby Foods**

You can save yourself a great deal of time if you purée one batch of meat or dessert course and divide it up into small containers (such as yoghurt cartons). Or freeze it in an ice cube tray, wrap cubes individually in foil and group in polythene bags. The food should be only lightly seasoned, and can be stored 3-4 months if necessary. Remember, as always when preparing baby foods, to be particularly careful about hygiene, and to sterilise all equipment.

**Bacon**

Freeze only bacon which is perfectly fresh. Smoked bacon can be stored longer than unsmoked before there is a risk of rancidity occurring. Pack rashers in ½ lb (250 g) quantities closely wrapped in foil or plastic film then overwrapped in polythene bags. If you buy vacuum-packed bacon joints or slices to freeze they can go into the freezer as they are.

RECOMMENDED FREEZER LIFE: rashers wrapped in foil and polythene: smoked, 8 weeks; unsmoked, 3 weeks; joints wrapped in foil and polythene: smoked, 8 weeks; unsmoked, 5 weeks. Vacuum packs, joints and rashers, smoked and unsmoked, 25 weeks.

TO USE: thaw overnight in fridge.

## Bamboo Shoots

Partially used cans of bamboo shoots freeze well in their own liquor. Transfer the contents to small cartons leaving ½in (1 cm) headspace and freeze.

RECOMMENDED FREEZER LIFE: 6 months.

TO USE: thaw overnight in fridge or for 4 hours at room temperature.

## Bananas

These do not freeze as a whole fruit but can be puréed and stored for use in bread or cake recipes or for sandwich fillings. Mix the purée with sugar and lemon juice and pack in small containers sufficient for immediate use.

RECOMMENDED FREEZER LIFE: 1 year.

TO USE: thaw overnight in fridge or 4 hours at room temperature.

## Batter

Prepare a Yorkshire pudding or pancake batter in the usual way. Pour ½ or 1 pt (250 or 500 ml) quantities into rigid containers, leaving ½-1 in (1-2 cm) headspace. Seal and freeze, remembering to keep the containers upright until batter is frozen.

RECOMMENDED FREEZER LIFE: 3 months.

TO USE: leave the batter to thaw for at least 2 hours.

See also *Pancakes* and *Yorkshire Pudding*.

## Beans, Lima

Young, tender broad beans freshly picked from the garden are an excellent freezer crop. Shell the beans and blanch

them for 2 minutes in boiling water. Cool in iced water or under a running tap. Drain, dry and pack in plastic bags.

If you prefer, spread the beans out on trays and freeze them, then tip into a polythene bag. Frozen in this way you can just tip out the amount you require each time.

RECOMMENDED FREEZER LIFE: 1 year.

TO USE: cook from frozen in boiling water.

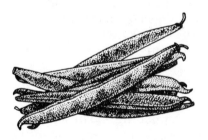

**Beans, Runner**

Pick young fresh beans, cut off the ends and string if necessary. Slice thickly, not into fine shreds or they will be flabby and tasteless when cooked. Blanch for 2 minutes. Cool, drain and open-freeze as for lima beans.

RECOMMENDED FREEZER LIFE: 1 year.

TO USE: cook from frozen in boiling water.

## Beans, String

These beans should be picked whilst young and thin when they will be tender and stringless and can be cooked whole. Wash them, trim the ends and blanch for 1-2 minutes. Cool, drain and open-freeze as for lima beans.

RECOMMENDED FREEZER LIFE: 1 year.
TO USE: cook from frozen in boiling water.

## Beef

If you are buying beef to freeze from your butcher ask for only first quality meat and make sure that it has been hung properly – anything from 6 to 12 days. The flesh of beef should be dull red and firm, the fat yellowish white. Good hanging is important for flavour and texture. Freezing won't improve quality or taste though it might tenderise slightly because the ice crystals break up the fibres.

If you are freezing the meat yourself here is the way to do it:

*Large cuts:* wipe meat with a damp cloth, trim off excess fat which tends to turn rancid if kept for a long time, make sure joints are of a usable size and preferably boned. Wrap closely in polythene or foil. Pad any sharp protruding bones with foil before wrapping.

*Steaks:* wipe with a damp cloth. Trim meat and wrap each steak in polythene or separate the steaks with a piece of waxed paper and pack in polythene bags.

*Ground:* discard as much fat as possible, grind meat and pack in small quantities (1lb or 2lb, 500g or 1kg) in polythene bags.

*Stewing meat:* cut into pieces and pack tightly in polythene bags to exclude as much air as possible. Use the discarded bones and lean meat trimmings to make beef stock.

*Uncooked meat:* meat that is to be marinaded or simmered, small cuts or chops, can be used straight from the freezer.

Steaks can either be cooked from frozen or thawed. If thawing, leave the beef in its wrappings and allow at least 5-6 hours in the refrigerator or 2½-3 hours at room temperature per lb (500g). For steaks allow 1-2 hours at room temperature.

If cooking a joint from frozen use the slow method of roasting and allow an extra 14-18 minutes per lb (500g).

*Cooked meat:* casseroles, stews, shepherd's pie, meat balls, meat sauces and steak and kidney pies can all be frozen in their cooked state. Cook stews and casseroles until just tender. Remove any surplus fat from the cooled surface before freezing. Check the seasoning when re-heating. Cook from frozen, re-heating at 350°F, 180°C, for 45 minutes.

*Sliced meat* to be eaten cold can be frozen with slices separated with waxed paper and packed tightly together in bags or cartons, or it can be frozen in foil dishes with its own gravy and thoroughly re-heated before eating. Thaw in fridge for 3 hours or 1½ hours at room temperature.

RECOMMENDED FREEZER LIFE: large cuts, 12 months; small cuts, 6 months; mince, 3 months; meat dishes, 3 months; sliced meat, 1 month.

## Beetroot

Ideally, freeze young beetroots. Wash them well and cook until tender. Rub off the skin, cool and pack in cartons. Freeze them whole or cut larger ones into dice or slices.

RECOMMENDED FREEZER LIFE: 6 months.

TO USE: thaw in the fridge.

## Biscuits/ Cookies

It is not worth freezing baked cookies as they store just as well in tins, but it's a good idea to have a roll of uncooked cookie dough in the freezer. In this way, you can have fresh cookies whenever you need them. Any cookie mixture containing over ¼lb (125g) fat to 1lb (500 g) flour will freeze satisfactorily.

Make up the cookie dough and shape it into one long sausage 2in (5 cm) across or several shorter sausages. Wrap in foil and freeze. To bake, put the wrapped roll in the refrigerator to soften slightly, then cut in ⅛-in (2.5-mm) slices and bake normally.

If you are using a soft cookie mixture pipe it into shapes on a baking tray and freeze uncovered. Lift the cookies off the tray with a palette knife and pack into polythene bags. These may be put on baking trays and baked straight from the freezer.

RECOMMENDED FREEZER LIFE: 6 months.

## Blackberries

These freeze extremely well – wild or cultivated ones – retaining their distinctive flavour from one season to the next. Wash the berries, if necessary, in a colander under the

21

cold water tap. Pat dry and pack in polythene bags. Pack and freeze. Use less than perfect fruit for purée. Wash the blackberries and put them into a saucepan with just the water that clings to them. Add sugar, about 4 oz (125 g) to 1 lb (500 g) fruit and stew gently. When fruit is tender, sieve, cool and pack in rigid containers, leaving ½-1 in (1-2 cm) headspace. Use later, thawed overnight in fridge or 3 hours at room temperature, for ice creams, mousses and sauces, or make into a dessert in the following way. Fill a mixing bowl with cubes of day-old crustless bread, and pour hot blackberry purée over the bread as you layer it into the basin. On top, put a plate which fits into the basin and on this put a 2 or 3 lb (1 or 1½kg) weight. Leave overnight in a cool place. Next day, turn out and serve with fresh whipped cream.

RECOMMENDED FREEZER LIFE: fruit and purée, 12 months.

TO USE: thaw overnight in fridge.

### Blackcurrants

Choose firm, ripe fruit to freeze whole and put hard or squashed currants aside for making juice. Stem the currants then wash if necessary and pat dry. Pack into polythene bags with or without sugar – about 6 oz (175 g) to 1 lb (500 g) fruit – and freeze. If preferred, spread currants out on tray, open-freeze and pack into polythene bags.

RECOMMENDED FREEZER LIFE: 1 year.

TO USE: thaw overnight in fridge or 3 hours at room temperature.

### Blackcurrant Juice

Use any surplus fruit, including the hard or squashed currants, to make blackcurrant juice, valuable as a winter drink because of its high vitamin C content.

Wash the currants, but don't bother to remove the stalks. Put into a saucepan with ½pt (300 ml) water to each 1 lb (500 g) fruit.

22

Bring quickly to the boil for 1 minute. Longer boiling will spoil the flavour and reduce the vitamin C content. Tip the fruit into a scalded jelly bag or muslin and let the juice drip through overnight.

Measure juice into a bowl and add ¾lb (300g) sugar to each 1pt (500ml) juice, stir until dissolved and pour into rigid containers leaving ½-1in (1-2cm) headspace to allow for expansion in freezing. Alternatively the juice can be frozen in ice cube trays, the cubes wrapped individually in foil and all stored in a polythene bag.

RECOMMENDED FREEZER LIFE: 1 year.

## Blueberries

Choose firm, ripe fruit, wash it and dry on kitchen paper. Place in a colander suspended over boiling water and steam blanch for 1 minute. This prevents the skin toughening. Cool and pack in polythene bags or rigid containers. If packed with sugar, crush berries slightly and mix with 4oz (125g) sugar to 1lb (500g) fruit. Pack in waxed cartons or other rigid containers leaving ½-1in (1-2cm) headspace for expansion. They can also be frozen in prepared syrup using ¾lb (300g) sugar to 1pt (500ml) water. As a rough guide you will need about ½pt (300ml) syrup for every 1lb (500g) fruit. Put fruit into waxed containers and cover with cold syrup. Leave ½-1in (1-2cm) headspace.

RECOMMENDED FREEZER LIFE: 1 year.

TO USE: thaw overnight in fridge or 4 hours at room temperature.

## Bouquet Garni

Make a quantity of these by tying together with white thread a sprig each of parsley and thyme with a bay leaf. Put the whole lot into a plastic bag or rigid container and freeze.

RECOMMENDED FREEZER LIFE: 1 year.

TO USE: take out when needed and use straight from the freezer in stews or casseroles.

## Brains

Wash the brains and pat dry. Remove as much skin and membrane as possible. Pack in 4 oz (100g) quantities in polythene bags and freeze.

RECOMMENDED FREEZER LIFE: 3 months.

TO USE: thaw overnight in fridge or 3 hours at room temperature.

## Brandy Butter

The traditional accompaniment to Christmas puddings and mince pies. Make it well ahead of time and store it in your freezer. Cream together 8 oz (250g) unsalted butter and 8 oz (250g) icing sugar. Then beat in brandy a little at a time. You will need about 6 tbs but taste as you go along. Pack in 4 or 8 oz (125 or 250g) quantities in rigid containers and freeze.

RECOMMENDED FREEZER LIFE: 2 months.

TO USE: it will take about 2 hours to thaw at room temperature.

## Bread

Most breads and bread doughs freeze well provided they are fresh when frozen.

*Bread* should be left in its packaging to thaw and will take from 3 to 6 hours according to the size of the loaf.

*Sliced bread* can be taken straight from the freezer and toasted while frozen.

RECOMMENDED FREEZER LIFE: 6 months.

*Bread dough:* all doughs can be frozen, preferably unrisen. Best results are obtained from doughs made with 50% more yeast than is given in the standard recipes. Freeze in 1-loaf quantities in heavy-duty polythene bags, lightly greased, and seal tightly.

RECOMMENDED FREEZER LIFE: plain dough, 3 months; enriched (milk or butter added), 4 months.

TO USE: Unseal bag, tie loosely, thaw and rise 5-6 hours at room temperature.

*Part-baked loaves and rolls* bought from a shop can be frozen as soon as you get them home.

RECOMMENDED FREEZER LIFE: 4 months.

TO USE: bake from frozen.

*Soft bread and rolls:* pack in polythene or foil.

RECOMMENDED FREEZER LIFE: 3 months.

*Crusty bread and rolls:* pack in polythene or foil.

RECOMMENDED FREEZER LIFE: 1 week (after which crust flakes).

*Brioches:* wrap in foil or polythene bags.

RECOMMENDED FREEZER LIFE: 2 months.

*Flavoured bread:* for garlic- or herb-flavoured bread (useful timesaver for last-minute dinner parties) use French or Vienna loaves. Slice the bread to within ½in (1 cm) of the bottom. Spread creamed butter flavoured with garlic or herbs between the slices. Wrap in heavy-duty foil and freeze. When ready to use put the wrapped and frozen loaf into the oven (400°F, 200°C) and heat: 30 minutes, French bread; 40 minutes, Vienna loaf.

RECOMMENDED FREEZER LIFE: 1 week.

*Fried bread:* croûtons for soup and fried bread shapes for canapés freeze well. Pack in polythene bags. Thaw uncovered in a hot oven for 5 minutes.

RECOMMENDED FREEZER LIFE: 1 month.

See also *Croissants*.

## Breadcrumbs

Prepare these in quantity for use in stuffings, puddings, for coating foods and for bread sauce. Pack them into polythene bags and freeze. They remain separate when frozen so it's easy to take out just what you need.

RECOMMENDED FREEZER LIFE: 3 months.

TO USE: for stuffings, puddings and sauces use them frozen, but for coating foods for frying leave at room temperature for 30 minutes.

*Buttered crumbs:* melt 1 oz (25 g) butter in a frying pan and stir in 4 oz (100 g) fresh breadcrumbs. Fry slowly until golden. Cool and pack in polythene bags. Use as a topping for gratin dishes or mix with sugar to top sweet dishes.
RECOMMENDED FREEZER LIFE: 1 month.

## Bread Sauce

Ready-made bread sauce in the freezer will ease the cooking timetable when roast chicken or turkey is on the menu at holiday time.

Peel a medium-sized onion, stick 4 cloves into it and put in a saucepan with a pint (500 ml) of milk. Simmer at low heat and leave to steep for an hour. Remove the onion and stir in 4 oz (100 g) breadcrumbs. Season with salt and pepper and cook gently for 15 minutes. Cool and pack in rigid containers, leaving a little headspace, and freeze.
RECOMMENDED FREEZER LIFE: 1 month.

TO USE: thaw in the top of a double boiler, stirring in a little cream at the end.

## Broccoli

This freezes very well, retaining both flavour and colour. Choose tender stalks not more than 1 in (2 cm) thick. Trim off any large leaves and cut stems into even lengths. Blanch, not more than 1 lb (500 g) at a time, for 3 minutes. It is easiest to do this in a wire basket. Place the vegetables in a basket and lower it into a large saucepan of boiling water, blanch, lift out and plunge into ice-cold water. Drain and either pack the spears immediately in polythene bags or rigid containers, or open-freeze first.

RECOMMENDED FREEZER LIFE: 1 year.

TO USE: cook from frozen in boiling water.

## Brussels Sprouts

Choose small, firm sprouts, trim off any discoloured leaves, wash and blanch: 3 minutes for small and 4 minutes for medium. Cool immediately in ice-cold water, drain and freeze free-flow: spread the sprouts on a baking tray and freeze uncovered. Then pack in a polythene bag, seal and return to the freezer.

RECOMMENDED FREEZER LIFE: 1 year.

TO USE: cook from frozen in boiling water.

## Butter

Leave butter in its original wrapping and then overwrap in foil or a polythene bag as it is easily affected by other strong odours.

RECOMMENDED FREEZER LIFE: unsalted butter, 6 months; salted butter, 3 months.

TO USE: thaw overnight in the refrigerator.

*Butter shapes:* you can prepare butter balls, curls or fancy shapes for parties, freeze them and store in polythene bags or rigid containers.

RECOMMENDED FREEZER LIFE: 3-6 months.

TO USE: thaw at room temperature for 10-15 minutes.

## Buttermilk

This can be frozen. It tends to separate on thawing, but a quick stir soon puts that right.

RECOMMENDED FREEZER LIFE: 6 weeks.

TO USE: thaw overnight in fridge.

## Butters, Savoury

These give the finishing touch to any number of cooked dishes and are made quite simply by working chopped herbs or other flavourings and seasonings into creamed butter. The following are probably the most widely used.

*Parsley (Maître d'hôtel) butter:* 8oz (250g) butter, 4-6 tbs finely chopped parsley, a squeeze of lemon juice, salt and pepper. Use with steak, fish and broad beans.

*Mint butter:* 8oz (250g) butter, 8 tbs finely chopped mint, a teaspoon lemon juice, salt and pepper. Use with lamb cutlets, peas and new potatoes.

*Mustard butter:* 8oz (250g) butter, 3tbs French Mustard, salt and pepper. Use with boiled ham, liver and grilled fish.

Work the butter and flavourings together, shape into a roll and wrap in freezer paper, pack into a polythene bag and freeze.

RECOMMENDED FREEZER LIFE: 3 months.

TO USE: cut off the number of slices you need, re-wrap the still frozen roll and return it to the freezer.

## Buttercreams

These freeze well and a selection of different flavours – chocolate and coffee are particularly good as their flavours do not deteriorate – are useful for filling and icing cakes.

Any flavourings should be pure: vanilla pod, extract or sugar rather than a synthetic substitute as these tend to develop 'off' flavours.

RECOMMENDED FREEZER LIFE: 3 months.

TO USE: thaw at room temperature. An 8oz (250g) quantity will take 2-3 hours.

## Cabbage

This will freeze but as it is available all the year round it is scarcely worth the trouble or the freezer space. Red cabbage, however, is not always available so if you like it, it may be worth your while to freeze some.

Wash the cabbage thoroughly, shred it and blanch it in plenty of boiling water for 1½ minutes. Cool rapidly in ice-cold water, drain and pack in polythene bags and freeze.

Red cabbage can be served plainly boiled but is more usually braised with a little onion, vinegar and sliced apples to serve with venison, pork or sausages. It can be frozen after braising and re-heated most successfully. Use polythene bags for freezing it and throw them away afterwards, as it's difficult to rid containers of the smell.

RECOMMENDED FREEZER LIFE: 1 year for blanched; 6 months for braised.

TO USE: cook or re-heat from frozen.

## Cakes

When you are baking cakes, double or treble the quantities so that you have one cake for immediate use and another one or two for freezing. Avoid synthetic flavourings as they develop 'off' flavours during freezing, and go lightly with spices. Chocolate and coffee cakes freeze very well as do fruit cakes, although a rich fruit cake will keep just as well in a tin.

Cakes may be buttercream-iced and filled though they keep longer if they are not. If you are putting a topping of buttercream on the cake, freeze it unwrapped until the frosting has set, then pack into a box. Try to use one only slightly larger than the cake to avoid drying during storage.

If you need sliced cake for packed lunches cut the whole cake into portions, put pieces of waxed paper between the portions, freeze the whole cake and just remove a slice as it is needed.

Small cakes can be packed in polythene bags in convenient quantities, but if they are iced they are better packed in boxes.

Wrap sponge cake layers separately, or slip a piece of waxed paper between the layers before packing into a box or plastic bag. Do not fill with jam or fruit as these make the cake soggy. Swiss rolls are best rolled up in cornflour, not sugar, if they are being frozen unfilled.

Buttercream freezes very well but boiled icings like American frosting, soft meringue icing and custard cream fillings do not freeze satisfactorily. (See *Icings*.)

RECOMMENDED FREEZER LIFE: plain cakes, 4 months; cakes with buttercream, 3 months.

TO USE: thaw sponge and layer cakes about 2 hours at room temperature; small cakes and buns, about 1 hour at room temperature.

Leave plain cakes to thaw in their wrappings, but unwrap iced cakes to prevent the wrapping sticking to the surface and spoiling the icing.

*Cake mixtures, unbaked:* Sponge and fruit cake mixtures can be frozen uncooked though there is little point in doing this unless there is time to mix them, but not bake them in the same session. Whisked sponge mixtures do not freeze well uncooked.

To freeze, line the tin the cake is to be baked in with foil, put in the mixture and freeze uncovered. Remove from the tin, wrap completely in foil, overwrap and return to the freezer. When baking, remove wrappings but leave in foil lining. Place frozen in a pre-heated oven and bake, allowing a slightly longer baking time than usual.

Alternatively the mixture can be frozen in rigid containers, allowed to thaw at room temperature for 2-3 hours then put into a cake tin and baked.

RECOMMENDED FREEZER LIFE: 2 months.

## Candied Peel

This keeps beautifully fresh and moist in the freezer and can be frozen in large pieces or chopped. Pack tightly in foil or polythene bags.

RECOMMENDED FREEZER LIFE: 1 year.

TO USE: thaw at room temperature for 3 hours.

## Canned Foods

If you use a lot of canned foods it is often cheaper to buy the catering sizes now widely available. When you open a can, divide the remaining contents into the serving portions you will require and freeze in rigid containers. Do not put the cans themselves in the freezer.

If liked, canned stewing steak or mince can be made into pies or pasties and frozen uncooked. But do this immediately, don't leave the opened cans standing around. You may notice a loss of texture in some of the products.

RECOMMENDED FREEZER LIFE: meats, 2 months; fruits, 6 months.

## Capons

These are young cockerels which have been caponised – that is, deprived of their male characteristics – by means of a simple and painless injection. They fatten easily and the flesh is fine and white. They are ideal for the freezer, being choice and tender birds, perfect for roasting for a family meal.

31

If it hasn't been done already, truss and tie the legs of the bird to the body. Do not stuff before freezing. Pack in polythene bags, extracting as much air as possible, and freeze.

RECOMMENDED FREEZER LIFE: 10 months.

TO USE: thaw for 24 hours in the refrigerator.

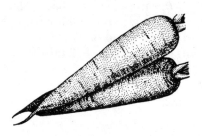

## Carrots

Although carrots are available all the year round, if you grow your own pull some of the baby carrots early and spare a little freezer space for them. They will be much appreciated later in the year and taste quite delicious when cooked with a little stock, butter and sugar.

Remove tops, wash and scrape them and leave whole if small. If not, cut into dice or rings. Blanch whole carrots for 3 minutes, dice or rings for 2 minutes. Cool in ice-cold water, drain and pack loosely in polythene bags. To keep the carrots separate, lay the bags flat in the freezer and when the carrots are frozen pack them more closely and seal.

RECOMMENDED FREEZER LIFE: 1 year.

TO USE: cook from frozen in boiling water or in butter and a little stock.

## Casseroles

It's well worth preparing these in quantity so that you've a meal for immediate use and several more safely tucked away in your freezer, for not much more effort than it takes to prepare one dish. Use any favourite recipe but for freezing remember that you will only need to cook the casserole for about three quarters of the usual time – the re-heating will finalise the cooking. Make sure there is plenty of sauce to cover the meat or it may dry out. Root vegetables, other than onions, are best added towards the end of the cooking time as they tend to go mushy. Don't season too heavily as this can be adjusted when re-heating, and if you are using garlic it is better to add this when re-heating as it tends to develop an 'off' flavour after about a week in the freezer.

When the casserole is cooked and cooled remove any surplus fat from the surface before freezing.

RECOMMENDED FREEZER LIFE: 6 weeks if bacon, ham or pork are used; 4 months for other meats.

TO USE: re-heat slowly from frozen.

## Cauliflower

Choose only first-class cauliflowers with firm, white, compact heads for freezing. Strip off any leaves. Wash the cauliflower and break into small sprigs about 2 in (5 cm) in diameter. Small heads may be left whole. Blanch in a large saucepan of boiling water for 3 minutes, or 4 minutes for small heads. Drain, cool and open-freeze on baking trays, pack into polythene bags and freeze.

RECOMMENDED FREEZER LIFE: 6 months.

TO USE: cook from frozen in boiling water.

## Celeriac

This is a root vegetable with a pronounced flavour of celery. It can be stored in a cool place throughout the winter, but as it also freezes excellently it is perhaps worth having some in the freezer, already prepared and blanched or puréed.

Peel the celeriac and cut into largish dice; blanch in boiling water for 4 minutes, cool, drain and pack in polythene bags.

*Purée:* peel the celeriac, cut it up roughly and put into a saucepan with stock - ¾ pint (450 ml) stock to 2 lb (1 kg) celeriac – and simmer until stock is absorbed. Purée in a blender or through a sieve. Cool, pack in rigid containers and freeze.

RECOMMENDED FREEZER LIFE: 1 year.

TO USE: serve the blanched celeriac boiled or braised. Serve the purée heated with butter and seasoning as a vegetable, or mixed half and half with mashed potato. Also as a soup thinned with creamy milk and seasoned.

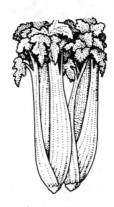

## Celery

Use crisp, tender stalks, remove any tough fibres and wash well to remove all dirt and grit. Cut in 2-in (5-cm) pieces and blanch for 3 minutes in boiling water. Cool, drain and pack in polythene bags and freeze.

Celery cannot be used raw after freezing but is useful as a vegetable, boiled or braised, or for use in stews and soups.

RECOMMENDED FREEZER LIFE: 1 year.

## Cheese

Hard cheese freezes very well and Cheddar, Cheshire, Double Gloucester, Edam and Gouda will all store for 6 months. A whole cheese or large wedge could therefore be a good buy. Divide it into convenient portions and pack closely in polythene bags pressing out surplus air. Make sure it is really well wrapped to prevent drying out and flavour transfer.

TO USE: leave in wrapping and thaw overnight in the refrigerator.

Blue cheeses freeze well but tend to crumble when thawed, though tests carried out on Stilton showed it was still creamy after several months in the freezer.

Cottage cheese is not suitable for freezing, both appearance and taste being unsatisfactory, but it can be used in made up dishes such as cheesecake, then frozen.

Cream cheese can be frozen for about 6 weeks, but after that time it tends to become yellow and hard, although again it is quite satisfactory used in made-up dishes and then frozen.

*Grated cheese:* this is useful to have for sauces and toppings. Grate a large quantity and pack into a polythene bag. It remains free-flowing and can be used straight from the freezer.

## Cheesecake

Cheesecakes, baked or unbaked, on a biscuit crust freeze very well. Line the tin to be used – preferably a loose-bottomed one – with foil. Make up any standard recipe, turn the mixture into the tin and chill until firm. Place in freezer, uncovered, until frozen. Remove from the tin, wrap completely in foil, overwrap in polythene bag and seal before returning to the freezer. If using fruit toppings or whipped cream decorations put these on after thawing.

RECOMMENDED FREEZER LIFE: 1 month.

TO USE: thaw at room temperature 4-6 hours.

## Cheese Sauce

If you use this regularly it's probably a good idea to make it up in bulk and freeze in ½ pint (250 ml) and 1 pint (500 ml) containers. Make up a good white sauce and add about 6 oz (150 g) strong Cheddar, grated, to each pint (500 ml) of sauce. Cool quickly, stirring occasionally to prevent a skin forming and freeze in rigid containers leaving ½ in (1 cm) headspace.

RECOMMENDED FREEZER LIFE: 3 months.

TO USE: heat gently, preferably in a double boiler so that it doesn't boil and spoil the texture, and stir well to prevent separation.

## Cherries

Both sweet and sour cherries freeze well but the red varieties are better than the black. Choose sound, ripe fruit, remove the stalks, wash and dry the fruit and take out the stones. The cherries can be left unpitted, but the fruit then tends to acquire an almond-like flavour. To freeze, spread the cherries on a baking tray and when frozen pack into polythene bags.

Or freeze in syrup: make up a syrup, using 8-10 oz (200-250 g) sugar to 1 pint (500 ml) water, depending on tartness of cherries, by heating the sugar and water together until dissolved, bringing to boil and leaving to become cold.

Put the cherries into rigid containers, cover with the prepared syrup, leaving ½-1 in (1-2 cm) headspace for expansion, and freeze. If necessary, a piece of crumpled waxed paper may be put on top of the fruit to hold it under the syrup before sealing.

RECOMMENDED FREEZER LIFE: 1 year.

TO USE: thaw at room temperature for 3 hours.

## Chestnuts

The preparation of fresh chestnuts is tedious and time-consuming but with a freezer you can do the job well before Christmas.

Choose heavy nuts with tight-fitting shells – a sign of freshness. Wash the nuts, make a small slit in the shells. Put a few in a saucepan, cover with cold water, then boil about 5 minutes. Take the pan off the heat, remove the chestnuts, put the next lot on to boil while shelling and skinning the first batch. Pop any reluctant to part with their inner brown skins back into boiling water for a further minute. When completed either pack the chestnuts in polythene bags and freeze, or cook them until soft, about 45 minutes, and make the stuffing to any standard recipe. Cool it and pack in rigid containers to freeze.

RECOMMENDED FREEZER LIFE: 6 months.

TO USE: thaw in the refrigerator for 12 hours.

As an alternative to boiling, peeling and skinning, dried chestnuts are useful and can be bought at health food shops and some large grocery stores.

## Chicken

It's not worth bothering to freeze anything other than plump, young, tender birds. Old birds are best cooked and the meat then made into pies, the bones into stock, or casseroled and then frozen.

Bought ready-frozen chickens should be put in the freezer as soon as possible after buying.

If you are freezing your own poultry starve them for 24 hours before killing to empty the crop. Pluck immediately after killing as the feathers come out more easily while the body is still warm. Then hang, head downwards, for a day. Remove head, feet and wing tips and draw the bird. Wipe inside and out with a damp cloth. Leave in the fridge for 2-3 days before freezing to mature and gain flavour. Truss and tie the legs to the body. Don't use skewers as these will tear the wrappings; pad the legs with foil for the same reason. Pack in polythene bags, extracting as much air as possible, or wrap tightly in foil, and freeze. If the giblets are to be frozen, wash, dry and pack these separately in polythene bags. If liked, remove livers and freeze these separately to use for pâté.

Do not stuff the chickens before freezing as the stuffing inhibits thorough thawing.

*Chicken portions:* halve, quarter or joint the bird, wipe the pieces with a damp cloth and wrap each piece separately in waxed or freezer paper. Overwrap all pieces in a polythene bag and freeze. If preparing a number of chickens at a time you may prefer to package drumsticks together, wings together and so on.

RECOMMENDED FREEZER LIFE: chicken, 1 year; giblets, 2 months.

TO USE: chickens *must* be thawed properly before being cooked. A medium-sized chicken will take 24 hours to thaw in wrappings in the fridge or overnight at room temperature. Chicken joints: thaw in wrapping 4-6 hours in the fridge.

## Chicory

Use this as a braised vegetable after freezing; it won't be suitable for salads. Choose compact heads, discard any bruised outside leaves and trim the stalks. Blanch for 2 minutes. Cool and drain well. Pack in polythene bags or rigid containers and freeze.

RECOMMENDED FREEZER LIFE: 12 months.

TO USE: put chicory, still frozen, into a dish with a little butter and braise.

## Chillies

These small bright red peppers are grown in the tropics where they are used shredded to lend flavour to bland foods. They can be very fiery and are an essential ingredient in tabasco sauce and curry powder. To prepare for freezing trim off stalks and remove seeds, blanch for 2 minutes, cool, drain and open-freeze. Pack into a polythene bag, seal, label and return to freezer.

RECOMMENDED FREEZER LIFE: 3 months.

TO USE: thaw and use as required.

**Chips.** See *Potatoes*.

## Chives

Scissor-snip chives into the little plastic containers used for

individual portions of jam, or pack them a tablespoon at a time into foil and freeze.

RECOMMENDED FREEZER LIFE: 6 months.

TO USE: straight from the freezer with salads or salad dressings, soups or mixed into cream or cottage cheese.

## Chops

These can be cooked quite successfully from frozen, so a supply of them – pork, lamb and veal – means a quick meal at any time.

Interleave the chops with waxed or freezer paper for easy separation or open-freeze and pack in small quantities in polythene bags.

RECOMMENDED FREEZER LIFE: pork, 3 months; lamb, 6 months; veal, 6 months.

TO USE: to grill frozen chops place them 2 inches (5 cm) further away from the heat than usual until they are nearly cooked, then move close to the heat for final browning. To fry frozen chops, put in a greased pre-heated pan over low heat. When nearly cooked increase heat and brown meat on both sides. Gentle cooking is the key to success with frozen chops. If you prefer, and there's time, thaw chops in their wrappings overnight in the fridge and cook in the usual way.

## Choux Pastry

Make up the pastry to any standard recipe and when you have a smooth mixture of piping consistency, freeze either unbaked or baked.

To freeze, unbaked: line trays with non-stick paper and, using a large plain nozzle, pipe out small dots of paste for profiteroles, 3-in (7.5-cm) lengths for eclairs or in a 7-in (17.5-cm) diameter circle for a ring. Freeze uncovered and when frozen remove from the baking sheet and pack in polythene bags, foil or rigid containers.

To freeze, baked: grease baking trays and pipe mixture on to them as described above. Bake (425°F, 220°C) for 10-25 minutes according to size, till brown, firm and crusty. Freeze uncovered, then pack in layers in rigid containers.

RECOMMENDED FREEZER LIFE: unbaked, 3 months; baked, 6 months.

TO USE: unbaked – place frozen shapes on a greased baking sheet and bake (400°F, 200°C) allowing 5 minutes longer than for freshly made choux pastry. Baked – place frozen shapes on a greased baking sheet and refresh for 10 minutes (325°F, 170°C).

*Patty Shells:* fill with creamed fish, meat or mushrooms and chicken livers and serve hot. Sprinkle tops with grated cheese or a powdering of paprika.

*Sweet:* serve cold, filled with cream or ice cream and topped with chocolate or coffee icing or with hot chocolate sauce.

## Christmas Pudding

Don't bother to freeze the normal rich pudding. There is no point in taking up valuable freezer space when it will keep perfectly well on the kitchen shelf. If you make a lighter pudding, freeze it. Boil it first for 6 hours. When cold remove from bowl, wrap in greaseproof paper and foil. Freeze.

RECOMMENDED FREEZER LIFE: 4 months.

TO USE: thaw overnight. Replace pudding in its original bowl, well buttered, cover with buttered paper and foil. Boil 2-3 hours.

## Coconut

The flesh of a fresh coconut can be shredded or grated and frozen. Test for freshness by giving the nut a shake; if you can hear the milk lapping the sides then it's fresh. Pack shredded or grated flesh into small containers, moisten with its own milk and freeze. Or toast the coconut and freeze it.

RECOMMENDED FREEZER LIFE: fresh, 6 months; toasted, 2 months.

TO USE: thaw at room temperature 1-2 hours and use for curry dishes, in fruit salads, for cakes, fudge and icings.

## Cod's Roe

Fresh cod's roe, cooked, freezes well. It should be cut in ½-in (1-cm) slices and packed in a rigid container with freezer paper between the slices.

RECOMMENDED FREEZER LIFE: 1 month.

TO USE: dust with flour and fry gently from frozen in a little hot fat until well browned.

*Smoked cod's roe:* available at fishmongers and delicatessen shops, can be frozen or made into a delicious pâté - often called taramasalata - and stored in the freezer ready for use as a dip or spread.

Blend together 8oz (250g) smoked cod's roe, 1 tsp onion juice, 3 fl oz (100ml) olive oil, 2 tbs lemon juice and 2 slices crustless white bread soaked in a little cold water and squeezed dry. Pack into a foil container, cover and freeze.

RECOMMENDED FREEZER LIFE: 3 months.

TO USE: thaw in the refrigerator overnight.

## Coffee

Can be frozen provided it is absolutely fresh. Beans should be bought freshly roasted then packed into heavy-gauge polythene bags and tightly sealed to exclude all air. The same with ground coffee. Coffee bought in film packs can be frozen in those; no further packaging is necessary. Catering-size tins of instant coffee can be opened and packed in small quantities in heavy-duty polythene bags. Exclude as much air as possible, tightly seal and freeze.

Freeze strong liquid coffee in ice cube trays, wrap individually in foil and store in polythene bags in the freezer. Use for chilling iced coffee without diluting it.

RECOMMENDED FREEZER LIFE: freshly roasted beans, 1 year; film packs and re-packed instant, 3 months.

TO USE: can be used from frozen.

## Cold Meat

When you have left-over cooked meat or poultry that you don't want to use immediately it can be frozen in any of the following ways.

Chopped – particularly ham, chicken, turkey and beef, to be used in salads – and stored tightly wrapped in polythene bags.

Sliced – to be eaten cold. Interleave the slices with waxed paper and pack tightly in meal-sized packs to avoid drying out. Place in rigid containers and freeze.

Sliced in gravy – slice meat, put into foil dish, ensure there is sufficient gravy to cover the meat completely. Cover with foil and freeze.

Sliced and packed with sauce and vegetables for one-meal servings – arrange the meat on a foil plate with appropriate sauce: mint with lamb, apple with pork, together with vegetables: creamed potatoes, braised celery, frozen peas with a pat of butter on them, mushrooms etc. and closely cover plate with foil before freezing.

RECOMMENDED FREEZER LIFE: 2 months.

TO USE: thaw meat to be eaten cold in fridge in its container. Meat with gravy, sauces and vegetables should be heated from frozen (400°F, 200°C) for about 40 minutes. Loosen foil before heating.

## Crab

Shellfish is highly perishable and to be frozen successfully must be absolutely fresh. This means caught, cooked and frozen all on the same day.

Cool the cooked crabs, remove all the edible meat from the shell and either pack the brown and white meat in separate containers or arrange the meat for serving in the cleaned crab shells, cover with moisture-proof paper and overwrap in polythene bags and freeze.

RECOMMENDED FREEZER LIFE: 1 month.

TO USE: thaw 6-8 hours in the fridge.

## Cranberries

These red-berried fruits with a slightly bitter tang are probably best known in this country in the form of cranberry sauce to serve with roast turkey. Either freeze the whole berries or make into a sauce and freeze.

Choose firm red berries, discarding green or blemished fruit, stem them, wash and dry and freeze free-flow. To do this, spread berries on trays and freeze uncovered until hard, tip into a polythene bag and return to the freezer.

*Cranberry sauce:* dissolve 6oz (175g) sugar in ¼ pint (150ml) water and boil for 5 minutes. Add 1lb (500g) stemmed and washed fresh cranberries (or use frozen ones), simmer until soft. Cool and pack in rigid containers, leaving ½-1in (1-2cm) headspace and freeze. For a smooth sauce, simmer fruit, water and sugar together until tender, sieve, then pack and freeze as above.

RECOMMENDED FREEZER LIFE: 1 year.

TO USE: both fruit and sauce will thaw in 2-3 hours at room temperature. If liked a little port may be added to the sauce before serving.

## Cream

Cream with a butterfat content as low as 35% can be frozen, but the best results are obtained from a higher fat content. Clotted cream freezes very well and will keep for 12 months. 10% cream also freezes well, but the cream must be really fresh. Both can be frozen in the containers in which they are bought provided there is room for expansion.

Results of recent tests on freezing cream showed the most successful way of freezing double or whipping cream is to chill it thoroughly and then semi-whip it before freezing. If this isn't done the cream tends to separate and be heavy and grainy with a buttery taste. Alternatively a little sugar, 1 tsp to 5 floz (150ml), stirred into the cream before freezing seems to act as a stabiliser and help overcome any tendency to separate. Even so, cream should not be stored for more than 3 months. Pack into rigid containers or use the containers in which it was bought, leaving ½-1 in (1-2 cm) headspace for expansion. Cover, seal and freeze.

*Whipped cream rosettes:* cream whipped until it just holds its shape can be piped into rosettes on a foil-covered tray and open-frozen, then stored in rigid containers for use on puddings and cakes. The rosettes will take about 10 minutes to thaw at room temperature and should be placed in position while frozen.

RECOMMENDED FREEZER LIFE: clotted cream, 12 months; 10%, double and whipping, 3 months.

TO USE: thaw cream overnight in the fridge. When re-whipping take care as the cream thickens quickly at this stage.

**Crêpes.** See *Pancakes.*

## Croissants

Freeze cooked croissants in polythene bags or, to give greater protection, in rigid containers. If you make your own croissants you can also freeze the unbaked dough. Prepare to the stage when all the fat has been added but do not give the final rolling. Wrap in polythene bag and freeze immediately.

RECOMMENDED FREEZER LIFE: unbaked dough, 6 weeks; baked croissants, 3 months.

TO USE: baked croissants, place frozen wrapped in foil in a moderate oven (350°F, 180°C) for 15 minutes. Unbaked dough, thaw in polythene bags, which should be undone and re-tied loosely so that the dough can rise, in the fridge overnight or at room temperature for 5 hours. Give final rolling, shape and bake.

### Croûtons

Those delicious tiny cubes of fried bread served with soups will freeze beautifully. Cube some day-old white bread without crusts and fry until golden, drain on absorbent paper and when cold pack into polythene bags, seal and freeze.

RECOMMENDED FREEZER LIFE: 1 month.

TO USE: thaw uncovered in a hot oven (425°F, 220°C) for 5 minutes.

### Crumble. See *Puddings*.

### Crumpets

These can be stored in the freezer in polythene bags.

RECOMMENDED FREEZER LIFE: 6 months.

TO USE: they can be toasted straight from the freezer or thawed for 6 hours in the pack.

### Cucumber

Because of its high water content cucumber will not freeze for use as a salad vegetable; it just goes mushy. It can, however, be frozen cooked. Prepare the cucumber by peeling it, quartering it lengthwise, removing the core, then cutting the rest into cubes. Put these in a colander, sprinkle with salt, a little wine vinegar and a pinch of sugar and leave to drain for about an hour. Use the drained cucumber to make soup or bake it with a little butter and herbs for about 30 minutes in a hot oven (425°F, 220°C), cool and freeze it.

RECOMMENDED FREEZER LIFE: 2 months.

TO USE: tip the frozen soup or baked cucumber into a saucepan and heat through gently.

## Curry

Any meat or poultry can be cooked and curried and frozen for later use, as can curry sauce. Make up your favourite sauce recipe using a bought curry paste or powder or, ideally, curry powder made with freshly bought and ground ingredients. Freeze in ½ or 1 pint (250 or 500ml) quantities, leaving ½-1 in (1-2 cm) headspace. Use with cooked meats, fish or hard-boiled eggs.

RECOMMENDED FREEZER LIFE: 3 months.

TO USE: re-heat gently, from frozen, in a saucepan, stirring regularly.

## Custard

There is little to be gained by freezing egg custard. It has to be cooked after freezing and may separate, so the dish might just as well be made up freshly. The same applies to caramel custard (crème caramel) and vanilla custard. Custard tart, which also has to be frozen raw, tends to have a poor flavour and taste of uncooked pastry, so it is not really suitable for freezing either.

# D

## Damsons

The skins of damsons are inclined to toughen during freezing and the stones flavour the fruit. For this reason they are best washed, halved and stoned then stewed and packed in rigid containers or puréed.

*Purée:* wash, halve and stone the fruit, cook gently in a little water until soft, sieve and sweeten to taste, 4oz (125g) sugar to 1lb (500g) fruit. Pour into rigid containers, leaving ½-1in (1-2cm) headspace and freeze.

RECOMMENDED FREEZER LIFE: 1 year.

TO USE: thaw at room temperature for 2-3 hours. Use the purée as a sauce, to make a mousse or mix it with lightly whipped cream and freeze to make a delectable ice cream.

## Danish Pastries

These can be frozen baked or the unbaked dough frozen in bulk.

*Unbaked dough:* prepare to the stage when all the fat has been added but do not give the final rolling. Wrap in a polythene bag and freeze.

*Baked:* pack when cold, iced or plain – the latter is better as they can be refreshed in the oven after freezing – in a rigid container or polythene bag. It is best to open-freeze iced ones.

RECOMMENDED FREEZER LIFE: unbaked dough, 6 weeks; baked pastries, 1 month.

TO USE: unbaked dough, thaw in polythene bag in the fridge overnight or at room temperature for 5 hours. The bag should be undone and re-tied loosely so that the dough can rise. Give final rolling, shape and bake.

*Bought pastries:* iced, leave in loosened packaging at room temperature for 1½ hours; plain, place frozen in moderate oven (350°F, 180°C) for 10 minutes.

**Dates**

Fresh dates may be frozen and as they have a limited season in the shops you may like to freeze some for later use. Remove the stones, pack the fruit into polythene bags or small cartons and freeze.

Dried dates may be frozen in the same way.

RECOMMENDED FREEZER LIFE: fresh and dried, 1 year.

TO USE: thaw at room temperature for 2 hours.

**Dips**

Savoury dips, such as those made with curd or rich cream cheese, cod's roe pâté or puréed eggplant may be frozen in readiness for a party. Go easy with the seasoning as this can be adjusted when the dip is thawed. Should they separate slightly when defrosted, stir them well before transferring to the serving dish.

RECOMMENDED FREEZER LIFE: 1 month.

TO USE: thaw overnight in the fridge or at room temperature for about 4 hours.

**Doughnuts**

Home-made or bought doughnuts can be frozen. Pack them in polythene bags in quantities to suit the family requirements. Exclude as much air as possible and seal.

RECOMMENDED FREEZER LIFE: 2 months.

TO USE: heat from frozen (400°F, 200°C) for 8 minutes.

**Dripping**

When making bulk buys of fresh meat use the trimmings of fat to render down into dripping. Chop it up roughly and spread out in a frying pan or roasting tin. Heat gently, pouring off the liquid fat as it's extracted. Pour into a square or rectangular container and when set divide into blocks and wrap in foil. Seal, label and freeze.

RECOMMENDED FREEZER LIFE: 6 months.

TO USE: thaw overnight in fridge.

**Duck**

Choose young ducks with pliable breastbones and flexible beaks for freezing. Older birds can be frozen but are probably best made into casseroles or pâtés first.

If you are freezing your own ducks prepare them in the same way as chicken. Starve them for 24 hours, kill them and pluck while still warm. Remove the head, feet and innards, wipe inside and out with a damp cloth and chill in the fridge before wrapping and freezing. Truss, but don't use skewers as they will tear the wrappings. Pad the legs with foil. Pack in polythene bag extracting as much air as possible and freeze. If the giblets are to be frozen, wash, dry and pack them separately in a polythene bag.

RECOMMENDED FREEZER LIFE: duck, 6 months: giblets, 2 months.

TO USE: thaw in wrappings in the fridge for 24 hours.

**Eclairs**

These – filled with whipped cream and topped with chocolate or coffee icing – should be frozen on trays and when hard, packed into rigid containers with a piece of foil between the layers.

RECOMMENDED FREEZER LIFE: 2 months.

TO USE: thaw at room temperature for 1 hour.

**Eggs**

Do not freeze hard-boiled eggs; the whites develop a leathery texture when frozen. Fresh eggs freeze very well, but they must be taken out of their shells.

*Whole eggs:* stir lightly with a fork to blend the white and yolk and add ½ tsp salt or sugar to every 6 eggs to prevent thickening. Pack into waxed container labelling carefully as to quantity and whether salt or sugar has been added. Or they can be frozen in ice cube trays. Mix as above, pour into the tray, put the dividers in place and freeze. Transfer the frozen cubes to a polythene bag. Don't forget to make a note of how many cubes equal one egg.

*Yolks:* mix as above with a little salt or sugar and freeze in small cartons carefully labelled or in ice cube trays. One tbs yolk = one egg yolk.

*Whites:* these can be frozen just as they are – no beating, no additions. Pack into small cartons and mark the quantity on the container. Two tbs white = one egg white.

RECOMMENDED FREEZER LIFE: 6 months.

TO USE: thaw at room temperature for 40 minutes. If egg whites are being used for meringues they can be broken up, thawed and beaten in one operation in mixer.

### Fat

Fat tends to turn rancid if kept frozen for any length of time, so it is as well to trim meat of any excess fat before freezing. Stews should be cooled and as much fat as possible skimmed from the surface before being frozen.

### Fats

Butter, margarine, lard, cooking fat can all be frozen provided they are well wrapped.

RECOMMENDED FREEZER LIFE: 5 months.

## Fennel

This is one of the earliest known herbs. It is a perennial with a tall bushy growth, strong shiny stems and feathery leaves. The leaves have an aniseed flavour and can be added to soups and sauces and used in fish dishes. They can be chopped and packed in small containers for freezing.

*Florence fennel* is a vegetable and it, too, has an aniseed flavour. To freeze it cut off the hard base and trim off any tough outer stalks. Cut the rest into short lengths, blanch for 3 minutes, cool, drain and pack into polythene bags.

RECOMMENDED FREEZER LIFE: 6 months.

TO USE: add the herb to fish dishes and sauces; cook the vegetable from frozen in boiling water until tender. Serve with a white or cheese sauce.

## Figs

*Fresh:* these should be soft and fully ripe. Wash gently to avoid bruising. Remove the stems. They can be open-frozen before being packed into polythene bags, or peeled, halved or sliced, packed into rigid containers and covered with cold syrup - ½lb (250g) sugar to 1pt (600ml) water and ¾tsp ascorbic acid. Ascorbic acid (vitamin C) can be bought in drug stores. Leave ½-1 in (1-2cm) headspace for expansion and hold fruit under the syrup with a piece of crumpled greaseproof paper. Seal and freeze.

*Dried:* these freeze well, retaining their moisture and freshness. Wrap in foil or polythene bags.

RECOMMENDED FREEZER LIFE: both fresh and dried figs can be frozen for 1 year.

TO USE: thaw at room temperature for about 2 hours.

## Fish

If you freeze fish at home it must be absolutely fresh, ideally caught and frozen on the same day, but certainly within 24 hours.

Prepare small fish, like mackerel, trout, herring, mullet by scaling the fish and removing the gut, gills and fins. Heads and tails can be left on. Wash thoroughly under running cold water and drain. Wrap closely in a polythene bag so that as much air as possible is excluded. Seal and freeze.

Large fish such as cod, haddock or halibut are best cut into fillets or steaks and made up into shallow packages. They freeze faster this way and are probably more useful as individual portions. Remove head, tail and fins, scrape the belly cavity, wash thoroughly under running cold water and drain. Either divide the fish into fillets or cut it across the bone into 1-in (2-cm) steaks. Wrap closely in a polythene bag, seal and freeze.

For serving whole, large fish such as a salmon or salmon trout can be frozen wrapped in heavy-gauge polythene or foil or ice-glazed. Scale the fish and gut it. Wash thoroughly under running cold water, drain and dry. Either package, seal and freeze or place unwrapped fish in freezer and leave until solid. Remove, dip in cold, fresh water when a thin film of ice will form over the fish. Return to freezer. Repeat about three times at half-hourly intervals. Wrap in heavy-gauge polythene and return to the freezer.

Dishes made with cooked fish like fish pie, fish cakes and kedgeree can be frozen and re-heated quite successfully.

RECOMMENDED FREEZER LIFE: for fish frozen at home: white fish, 3 months; oily fish, 2 months; cooked fish dishes, 1 month.

TO USE: small fish, fillets and steaks can be cooked from frozen. Thaw a whole salmon for 24 hours in a cool place. Cooked fish dishes can be re-heated from frozen.

See also entries for individual fish.

## Flans

When making pastry, double the quantities and use the extra to make a flan case for the freezer. In this way you will build up a stock of cases that are endlessly useful for speedy savoury and sweet dishes. They can be frozen unbaked or baked, unfilled or filled, whichever is easiest at the time.

*Unfilled, unbaked or baked:* freeze in flan ring or foil case until hard, remove ring or case and wrap in a polythene bag. Baked cases need protection against damage, so pack them in boxes.

*Filled:* make up any quiche or savoury flan, bake and cool then open-freeze so the surface doesn't get damaged. When frozen wrap in polythene bag and return to freezer.

Sweet flans can be frozen, too, but not meringue toppings; these should be added before serving.

RECOMMENDED FREEZER LIFE: unbaked, unfilled, 3 months; baked, unfilled, 6 months; baked, filled, 2 months.

TO USE: unbaked, unfilled: return flan case to its original container and bake blind (400°F, 200°C) for 20-25 minutes. Baked, unfilled: thaw at room temperature for about 1 hour. Baked, filled: loosen wrappings and thaw at room temperature for 2 hours to serve cold, or heat through (350°F, 180°C) about 20 minutes.


**Florence Fennel.** See *Fennel.*


## Frankfurters

Originating in Germany, these were traditionally served with sauerkraut or a hot potato salad, but they are just as good with coleslaw and sauté potatoes or as a kebab with mushrooms, onions and green peppers or with baked beans. Pack them into polythene bags to suit your family requirements and freeze. If you buy them vacuum-packed they can go straight into the freezer without further wrapping.

RECOMMENDED FREEZER LIFE: 3 months.

TO USE: thaw overnight in the fridge.

**Fruit.** See entries for individual fruits for details of how to freeze. See *Ascorbic Acid* for how to freeze without sugar.

## Fruit Salad

Any fruits suitable for freezing may be combined and frozen in syrup as a fruit salad. Try a mixture of sliced apples, orange segments, grapes, peeled and seeded, fresh or canned pineapple and melon cubes. Bananas, if used, should be added when the salad has thawed. A summer selection could be raspberries, currants and stoned sweet cherries.

To make the syrup: dissolve 8oz (250g) sugar in 1pt (600ml) water, bring to the boil, remove from the heat and leave to cool. This will give a medium-strength syrup, but use more or less sugar to suit your own taste. Add the juice of a lemon or ¼ tsp ascorbic acid to the syrup when freezing fruits such as apples, pears, peaches, apricots, cherries and plums to prevent browning.

Put the syrup into rigid containers and add the fruit as it is prepared. Leave ½-1 in (1-2cm) headspace and hold the fruit under the syrup with a piece of crumpled greaseproof paper, seal and freeze.

RECOMMENDED FREEZER LIFE: 1 year.

TO USE: thaw overnight in the fridge.

## Fudge

All kinds of fudge can be frozen. Pour the mixture into shallow rectangular foil containers, mark into squares when beginning to set. When cold, cover with foil, seal, label and freeze. Or cut into pieces and pack in rigid containers with waxed paper or foil between the layers. Seal, label and freeze.

RECOMMENDED FREEZER LIFE: 3 months.

TO USE: place on a dish or wire rack and thaw at room temperature for about ½ hour.

# G

## Game

All game freezes most successfully. It must be hung before freezing for the same length of time as it would be for immediate use. This time varies depending on the weather and individual taste, but is usually between 7 and 10 days. After hanging, pluck, draw and remove as much shot as possible, wipe inside and out with a damp cloth and truss as for a chicken. Pack into a polythene bag and freeze.

For further details refer to individual entries (*Partridge, Pheasant, Venison* etc.).

## Gâteaux

These are rich and luscious cakes for festive occasions and as such are time-consuming to make. But as they freeze beautifully, either whole or in parts – sponge bases, flavoured buttercreams, toasted nuts, chocolate shapes – they can be prepared well ahead of a party. If you prefer to freeze the completed cake do so the day it is made. Sandwich the sponge layers with buttercream, ice and decorate. Open-freeze until the icing has set, then place in a polythene bag and, for extra protection, in a rigid plastic container or cardboard box as well.

RECOMMENDED FREEZER LIFE: 3 months.

TO USE: take out of box and remove from polythene bag so that the icing doesn't stick to the bag during thawing. Leave at room temperature for 2-6 hours.

## Giblets

These have a shorter freezer life than poultry so should always be stored separately, packed in polythene bags. If liked, freeze the livers on their own for use in risotto or pâté and the rest of the giblets together for making into stock for gravy or soup.

RECOMMENDED FREEZER LIFE: 2 months.

TO USE: thaw in the fridge overnight and use as suggested.

## Glacé Fruits

These are a luxury but can often be had at bargain prices after Christmas, so stock up then and store them in your freezer where they will retain their moisture and freshness for a year. Leave in their original containers and overwrap or wrap each piece of fruit in foil and package together in a polythene bag.

RECOMMENDED FREEZER LIFE: 1 year.

TO USE: thaw in wrappings at room temperature for 3 hours and use as a dessert or in cakes and puddings.

## Goose

Choose a young bird without too much fat. They are usually sold ready for cooking, but if you are killing your own hang it for 5 days before freezing. Pluck it, draw it and wipe inside and out with a damp cloth. Truss the bird, cover the bones with foil and pack in a polythene bag, extracting as much air as possible, and freeze. Pack the giblets separately and freeze.

RECOMMENDED FREEZER LIFE: 4 months – goose is a rich fatty meat and doesn't have a long freezer life. Giblets, 2 months.

TO USE: thaw in wrappings in the fridge allowing 24-36 hours.

## Gooseberries

Choose firm, ripe fruit – unless it is being stored for jam-making when it should be slightly underripe – wash, dry, top and tail and freeze whole or as a purée.

*Whole:* pack into polythene bags without sugar for use later in pies, crumbles or stewed or for making jam.

*Purée:* stew fruit – no need to top or tail – with a little water to prevent catching and sugar – 4-6oz (125-175g) to a lb (500g) of fruit–until soft. Sieve, cool and freeze in rigid containers, leaving ½in (1cm) headspace. Use for fools, mousses, ice cream.

RECOMMENDED FREEZER LIFE: 1 year.

TO USE: the whole fruit can be cooked from frozen, the purée should be thawed overnight in the fridge.

## Grapefruit

It's worth freezing a supply of these when prices are low; they freeze well and make a refreshing, healthy start to a meal. Peel the fruit, removing all the pith with the skin. Cut into segments leaving the dividing membrane behind. Layer the fruit with sugar - 4-6oz (125-175g) to 1 lb (500g) fruit - into rigid containers and freeze.

Or prepare grapefruit and pack in sugar syrup. Make a heavy syrup by dissolving 1 lb (500g) sugar in 1 pint (600ml) water. Bring to boil, remove from heat and cool. Put the grapefruit segments into a rigid container and cover with the cold syrup. Leave ½-1 in (1-2cm) headspace, seal and freeze.

*Juice:* halve and squeeze juice from the fruit, taking care not to press too much or you'll get the pithy flavour into the juice and spoil it. Freeze sweetened or unsweetened in rigid containers, leaving ½-1 in (1-2cm) headspace.

RECOMMENDED FREEZER LIFE: 1 year.

TO USE: thaw overnight in the fridge.

## Grapes

These are always available, but a few frozen for use in fruit salads and jellies could be useful. Seedless grapes can be packed whole, others should be skinned, halved and pipped. Pack into rigid containers and cover with cold sugar syrup – 8 oz (250 g) sugar dissolved in 1 pint (600 ml) water, brought to the boil then cooled. Leave ½-1 in (1-2 cm) headspace. Seal and freeze.

RECOMMENDED FREEZER LIFE: 1 year.

TO USE: thaw at room temperature for about 2 hours.

## Green Plums

Choose firm, ripe fruit with no blemishes. Wash if necessary and dry. They can be frozen whole as a dry pack, but the skins tend to toughen and the stones flavour the fruit during long-term storage, so this method is not recommended except for short periods of up to 3 months. The most successful ways of freezing them are:

1. Halve, stone and pack in rigid containers with cold syrup – 8 oz (250 g) sugar to 1 pint (600 ml) water. Put a piece of crumpled greaseproof on top of the fruit to keep it under the syrup. Leave ½-1 in (1-2 cm) headspace for expansion, seal and freeze.

2. Halve, stone and stew the fruit. Pack in rigid containers, leaving ½-1 in (1-2 cm) headspace, seal and freeze.

RECOMMENDED FREEZER LIFE: 1 year.

TO USE: fruit in syrup can be cooked from frozen. Stewed fruit should be thawed at room temperature for about 2 hours.

## Grouse

Like all game, grouse must be hung before freezing for the same length of time as for immediate use. How long this is will depend on the weather and individual taste but will probably be 7-10 days. After this, pluck, draw and prepare it in the same way as a chicken. Pack in a polythene bag, extracting as much air as possible and freeze.

RECOMMENDED FREEZER LIFE: 6 months.

TO USE: thaw in fridge allowing 5 hours per lb (500 g). Young birds are best plainly roasted, older birds can be casseroled or made into pies or pâtés.

## Guava

This is a tropical fruit noted for its high vitamin C content. There are a number of species varying in colour when ripe from pale yellow to reddish purple. The former is the most commonly grown.

Freeze in purée form or washed, peeled and halved then cooked in a syrup of 8 oz (250 g) sugar to 1 pt (600 ml) water and frozen in the syrup in rigid containers. Leave ½-1 in (1-2 cm) headspace for expansion.

RECOMMENDED FREEZER LIFE: 1 year.

TO USE: thaw at room temperature for about 2 hours. Try combining it with pineapple or banana to improve its rather bland flavour.

## Guinea Fowl

When choosing a guinea fowl look for a bird with a plump breast and smooth-skinned feet. A freshly killed bird needs to be hung before plucking, at least 2 days in warm weather, longer in cold. Prepare as for chicken. Pack in a polythene bag, extracting as much air as possible and freeze.

RECOMMENDED FREEZER LIFE: 10 months.

TO USE: thaw in fridge for 24 hours. It may be braised, grilled, roasted or casseroled or cooked in any of the ways recommended for chicken or pheasant. The flesh is a little on the dry side so when roasting a young bird use plenty of fat.

## Haddock

*Fresh:* as with all fish, haddock must be absolutely fresh to be frozen at home. Remove head, tail and fins, scrape the belly cavity and wash thoroughly under running cold water, drain and dry. Divide the fish into fillets or cut it across the bone into 1-in (2-cm) steaks. Wrap closely in polythene bags and freeze. Or use special freezer-cooking bags: put a portion of fish together with some thick white sauce into each bag, seal and freeze.

*Smoked*: freshly smoked haddock can be frozen raw or cooked. Arrange with your fishmonger to let you have some frozen, if this is how he buys it. Wrap the fish closely in polythene bags and freeze.

RECOMMENDED FREEZER LIFE: fresh and smoked haddock, 2 months; cooked haddock, 1 month.

TO USE: both fresh and smoked haddock can be cooked from frozen; cooked dishes can be re-heated from frozen. Put the freezer-cooking bags containing fish and sauce into a pan of boiling water for about 20 minutes to cook fish and re-heat sauce.

See also *Kedgeree*.


## Halibut

The same applies to the freezing of halibut as to fresh haddock above. If, however, you prefer to keep the fish whole for serving stuffed and baked, it can be frozen wrapped in heavy-gauge polythene or foil or ice-glazed.

Scale the fish and gut it. Wash thoroughly under running cold water, drain and dry. Either package, seal and freeze or ice-glaze. Place unwrapped fish in freezer until hard. Remove, dip in cold, fresh water when a thin film of ice will form over the fish. Return it to the freezer. Repeat about three times at half-hourly intervals. Wrap in heavy-gauge polythene or foil and return to the freezer.

RECOMMENDED FREEZER LIFE: 2 months.

TO USE: fillets and steaks can be cooked from frozen. Thaw a whole fish for 5-6 hours per lb (500g) in the fridge.

## Ham

This has a limited freezer life because the high salt content will make it turn rancid in a short time. It won't have gone bad but it won't taste very pleasant.

*Cooked ham* can be cut in thick slices separated by greaseproof paper then packed tightly in a polythene bag.

*Chopped ham* can be packed in polythene bags or rigid containers for use in salads or for vol-au-vent fillings.

*Uncooked ham* is best stored in the piece, closely wrapped in foil and overwrapped in a polythene bag.

RECOMMENDED FREEZER LIFE: cooked ham, sliced or chopped, 1 month; uncooked ham, 2 months.

TO USE: thaw in wrappings in fridge: sliced or chopped about 3 hours; in the piece, 5 hours per lb (500g).

## Hazelnuts or Filberts

Freeze hazelnuts to prolong their life – they will keep fresh and moist for a year. They can be frozen whole, chopped, flaked or toasted but should not be salted. Pack in foil or small cartons and freeze.

RECOMMENDED FREEZER LIFE: 1 year; 4 months buttered and toasted.

TO USE: thaw at room temperature for 3 hours.

## Hearts

These can be frozen raw or cooked. Trim off any fat and cut away blood vessels. Wash well in cold water, drain and dry. Pack in polythene bags and freeze. Or stuff and braise and freeze in rigid containers.

RECOMMENDED FREEZER LIFE: raw, 3 months; cooked, 2 months.

TO USE: raw, thaw in the fridge, allowing 5 hours per lb (500g); cooked, may be re-heated from frozen in a moderate oven.

## Herbs

Most herbs freeze well – mint, parsley, chives, tarragon are all excellent – so it's worth freezing any that you use regularly. They don't need blanching but should be washed and dried before freezing either whole or chopped.

*Whole:* pack sprigs of chosen herb into polythene bags and freeze. Tie sprigs of parsley, thyme and a bay leaf together for use where a bouquet garni is called for.

*Chopped:* chop herbs finely and freeze in the little plastic containers used for individual portions of jam or pack into ice cube trays, cover with water and freeze. Tip frozen cubes into a polythene bag and store in the freezer.

RECOMMENDED FREEZER LIFE: 6 months.

TO USE: add to stews and sauces straight from the freezer.

## Herrings

These should only be frozen if freshly caught. Scale the fish by scraping with a knife from tail to head. Rinse thoroughly then remove the gut, gills and fins. Head and tail can be left on. Wash well under running cold water and drain. Wrap each fish closely in a polythene bag, excluding as much air as possible, and freeze.

RECOMMENDED FREEZER LIFE: 2 months.

TO USE: cook from frozen.

## Hollandaise Sauce

This is not a sauce to freeze at home. It is made of butter and egg yolks acidulated with lemon juice or vinegar. It separates when frozen and thawed and you can't get it back to the right consistency.

## Horseradish

If you have a root of horseradish in the garden you can make up a supply of horseradish cream for the freezer. Grate the horseradish and mix it with lemon juice and sugar. Fold it into whipped double cream, pack in rigid containers and freeze. Quantities are: 2 tbs grated horse-radish, 2 tsp lemon juice, 2 level tsp sugar to a ¼ pt (150 ml) double cream.

RECOMMENDED FREEZER LIFE: 2 months.

TO USE: thaw in the fridge for 6 hours.

## Ice Creams

Any favourite recipe can be made and stored in the freezer. The mixture freezes more quickly than when made in the fridge and doesn't need stirring.

Whether you make your own or buy commercial ice cream don't store it too long because it tends to become grainy.

Flavourings for ices should be pure rather than synthetic essences. Fruit purées combined with cream make the most delicious ices. They are best freshly made so keep a stock of purées – raspberry, strawberry, blackcurrant, apricot – in the freezer and make them as you need them. Thaw the purée and fold it into lightly whipped cream, tip into a mould or plastic box and freeze.

Allow the ice to thaw a little before serving. It's unpleasant to eat when still hard and lacking in flavour. The time will vary depending on the ice, the container and how soft you like it. About 1 hour in the fridge for a fruit and cream ice, 30 minutes for a sorbet or water ice is a rough guide. Ices made with evaporated milk usually take a little longer to thaw than those made with cream.

RECOMMENDED FREEZER LIFE: commercial ice cream,

1 month; home-made ice cream and sorbets, 2 months.
TO USE: thaw to soften.

## Icings

Buttercream icing freezes very well and a selection of flavours (chocolate and coffee are particularly good as their flavours do not deteriorate) is useful for filling or icing cakes.

Boiled icings and egg-white icings like American frosting, soft meringue icing and royal icing tend to crumble on thawing so are not recommended.

Cakes can be filled and iced with buttercream and then frozen. To avoid damaging the iced surface, open-freeze them. When hard pack into polythene bags and return to the freezer. Unwrap before thawing.

Glacé-iced cakes can also be frozen successfully.
RECOMMENDED FREEZER LIFE: 3 months.

TO USE: thaw iced cakes at room temperature about 2 hours; thaw buttercream icing at room temperature. An 8 oz (250 g) quantity will take 2-3 hours.

## Jam

When there is a glut of fruit and no time to turn it into jam, store it in the freezer for a more convenient moment. Choose sound fruit, prepare and pack it in suitable quantities and freeze. Add one-eighth extra weight when freezing fruits that tend not to set too well. Follow the original recipe for sugar and yield.

When making jam from frozen plums and damsons, the skins of which toughen with freezing, the following method is recommended.

Bring the amount of water given in the recipe to the boil and add the frozen plums or other fruit a little at a time. This rapid thawing helps to soften the skins.

Then follow the recipe as for fresh fruit.

Blackcurrants should be blanched for 1 minute and cooled before packing and freezing to prevent the skins toughening. Alternatively they may be treated as the stone fruits above.

RECOMMENDED FREEZER LIFE: 1 year.

TO USE: follow method for stone fruits otherwise put the frozen fruit in a preserving pan with water if required, heat very gently until the fruit is thawed then make the jam following the method for fresh fruit.

## Jellies

Clear jellies are not good freezer material. They become granular and cloudy with storage.

Packet jellies made up with evaporated milk are, however, satisfactory and so is gelatine used in a creamy mousse mixture.

**Jerusalem Artichokes.** See *Artichokes, Jerusalem.*

## Kale

Pick young, tender leaves, remove from stems and wash well. Blanch for 3 minutes, cool and drain. Pack into polythene bags in quantities suitable for family requirements and freeze.

RECOMMENDED FREEZER LIFE: 1 year.

TO USE: cook from frozen in boiling water for 8 minutes.

## Kebabs

Lean leg of lamb or pork cut into cubes together with squares of green pepper, button mushrooms, whole baby onions or slices of onion can be prepared for kebabs, marinaded and frozen. Put the meat and vegetables in a shallow dish and pour over them a mixture of red or white wine, olive oil, seasonings and herbs. Leave to marinade for 2 hours. Thread the ingredients on to skewers – wooden or stainless steel – pad the sharp ends, wrap each skewer in foil and overwrap several skewers in a polythene bag and freeze. Put the marinade in a rigid container and freeze. Or pack the meat and vegetables, unskewered, into rigid containers, pour over the marinade, seal and freeze.

RECOMMENDED FREEZER LIFE: lamb kebabs, 3 months; pork kebabs, 2 months.

TO USE: thaw marinade and use to baste kebabs. Cook skewered kebabs from frozen; thaw unskewered kebabs and marinade overnight in the fridge.

## Kedgeree

This combination of rice and smoked haddock freezes very successfully and is a good stand-by dish to have.

Use 1 lb (500g) of smoked haddock to 6oz (185g) long grain rice. When cooked flake the haddock into the rice, stir in 1oz (30g) butter and 2tbs chopped parsley. Pack into polythene bags or dot the base of foil freezer dishes with butter and spoon in the kedgeree. Seal and freeze.

RECOMMENDED FREEZER LIFE: 1 month.

TO USE: from polythene bags: melt a little butter in a wide saucepan, tip the frozen mixture on to it, heat gently, breaking it up with a fork. When hot, season and stir in chopped hard-boiled egg. From freezer dishes: loosen the covering but leave in position. Heat through (400°F, 200°C) for about 45 minutes, stirring occasionally. Season and garnish with hard-boiled egg.

## Kidneys

Fresh kidneys should have the fat and thin skin removed and be washed and dried before freezing. Spread them on a tray and open-freeze then pack them in a polythene bag, or interleave them with waxed paper, overwrap in polythene bags and freeze.

Ready-frozen kidneys must be put in the freezer immediately after being bought.

RECOMMENDED FREEZER LIFE: 3 months.

TO USE: fry gently from frozen after removing cores, if not done before freezing and halving, or thaw and use as required.

## Kippers

Freshly smoked kippers may be frozen. Make sure they are well wrapped as their strong smell may be absorbed by other foods in the freezer.

RECOMMENDED FREEZER LIFE: 2 months.

TO USE: cook from frozen.

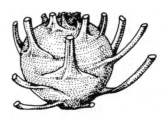

## Kohlrabi

Use young tender roots 2-3 in (5-7.5 cm) in diameter. Cut off tops and wash. Small ones, no more than 2 in (5 cm) in diameter, can be left whole, unpeeled but scrubbed and blanched for 3 minutes; older and larger ones should be peeled, diced and blanched for 2 minutes. Cool and drain. Open-freeze on trays, when hard pack in a polythene bag or pack required amounts in polythene bags and freeze.

RECOMMENDED FREEZER LIFE: 1 year.

TO USE: cook from frozen in boiling water.

## Kumquats

These fruits, looking like very small oranges, have a bittersweet flavour and can be frozen dry (packed in foil or polythene bags) or in sugar syrup, skins and all. Sugar syrup: pack fruit into rigid containers, cover with cold sugar syrup – 8oz (250g) sugar to 1pt (600ml) water – leave ½-1in (1-2cm) headspace, seal and freeze.

RECOMMENDED FREEZER LIFE: dry pack, 2 months; syrup pack, 12 months.

TO USE: thaw overnight in the fridge or about 3 hours at room temperature.

Kumquats can be added to fruit salad or marmalade and used as a filling for pavlova.

## Lamb

This is a good buy for the freezer. An average lamb carcass weighs about 30lb (15kg) and will give you a variety of cuts for roasting, grilling and stewing.

Provided you are prepared to use the scrag end and breast there is considerable saving in bulk-buying. Your local butcher is probably the best person to supply it; he'll joint the carcass to suit your requirements. You may like to have the best ends formed into a crown roast for a special dinner or it may suit you better to have them divided into cutlets or noisettes. If your family is small, each shoulder could be divided into two joints. Many butchers will package and label meat too so it's freezer-ready. If you package yourself, wrap closely round the meat, extracting as much air as possible before sealing. Chops can be open-frozen on a tray before being packed in polythene bags, or interleaved with waxed paper for easy separation.

Don't freeze more than a tenth of your freezer capacity in any 24 hours.

RECOMMENDED FREEZER LIFE: 6 months.

TO USE: cook from frozen or thaw the meat slowly in fridge allowing about 5 hours per lb (500g). The recommended time for roasting frozen lamb (350°F, 180°C) is 60 minutes per lb (500g). To grill frozen chops, place meat 2 in (5cm) further from heat than usual; when almost cooked place nearer the heat to brown.

## Lard

This keeps well in the fridge, but can be frozen too, provided it is well wrapped.

RECOMMENDED FREEZER LIFE: 5 months.

TO USE: thaw in the fridge overnight.

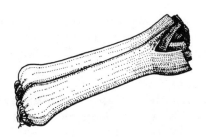

## Leeks

These are not always available but are so useful for soups, stews or simply as a vegetable that it's worth having a few packs in the freezer.

Choose young, even-sized leeks. Trim off green tops, root ends and any coarse outer leaves and wash thoroughly to get rid of all the earth. This is best done by slitting the leeks down the top for 2 or 3 in (5-6cm) and running cold water through the leaves. Blanch whole for 3 or 4 minutes according to size, cool, drain and pack in polythene bags.

Cut thicker ones into slices and blanch for 2 minutes, cool, drain and freeze in ½lb (250g) quantities in polythene bags.

RECOMMENDED FREEZER LIFE: 6 months.

TO USE: cook from frozen in boiling water 7-10 minutes;

add sliced frozen leeks to stews. Or make into soup: soften the still-frozen sliced leeks in 1 oz (30g) butter for 5 minutes, then add any other vegetables being used, stock and seasoning and simmer gently until cooked. Sieve or liquidise.

## Lemons

Always available but cheaper at certain times of the year, particularly in street markets. Then is the time to buy and freeze them. Whole for later use in marmalade; or juice and peel packed separately for use in drinks, ices, cakes, puddings; or sliced to use in drinks or as a garnish. You can also make lemon curd to freeze. It has a limited shelf life – about 6 weeks – but will keep beautifully in the freezer for 6 months.

*Whole fruit:* wash and dry, wrap closely in polythene bags and freeze.

*Juice:* halve and squeeze juice from fruit, taking care not to press too much or you'll get the pithy flavour into the juice and spoil it. Freeze sweetened or unsweetened in rigid containers or ice cube trays. If using the latter, pack cubes into polythene bags when frozen.

*Peel:* grate peel before squeezing out juice, pack into small cartons. Or simply pack the ½ lemons from which you have squeezed the juice into polythene bags. When rind is needed, grate the required amount from frozen.

*Slices:* wash and dry lemons, cut into slices, spread on a tray and open-freeze. When hard, pack into polythene bags and return to freezer.

RECOMMENDED FREEZER LIFE: 1 year.

TO USE: whole fruit: use frozen following a whole fruit recipe for marmalade. Juice: thaw and use as required. Peel: use from frozen for flavouring. Slices: use frozen in drinks, but thaw at room temperature for about 1 hour if using as a garnish.

## Lettuce

Because of its high water content, lettuce will not freeze and thaw satisfactorily for use in salads. It can, however, be

braised or made into soup and frozen and this would be a good way to use up a surplus supply from the garden.

## Limes

It's worth freezing the juice for drinks or making into sorbets or water ices. Slices could be frozen, too, for use in drinks or as a garnish. See *Lemons* for how to freeze.

RECOMMENDED FREEZER LIFE: 1 year.

TO USE: juice: thaw and use as required. Slices: use frozen in drinks, but thaw at room temperature for about 1 hour if using as a garnish.

## Liver

Rich in iron, this is an excellent family food and freezes well, raw or cooked. Wash it thoroughly, removing any blood and pipes, and dry. Cut into slices, interleave with waxed paper and pack in quantities suitable for family requirements in polythene bags; freeze.

If freezing cooked liver, pack the slices in a foil container and make sure they are covered with sauce or gravy. Cover and freeze.

*Chicken livers:* cut off any greenish marks from the bile sac, wash, dry and pack in small quantities in cartons or polythene bags.

RECOMMENDED FREEZER LIFE: raw, 3 months; cooked, 2 months.

TO USE: raw liver: thaw slices in fridge and as soon as they have begun to soften, separate and cook in the usual way. It should never be overcooked: when cut, the centre should be pinkish. Cooked liver: re-heat from frozen covered with foil. Chicken livers: thaw in fridge; when beginning to soften, use as required.

## Lobster

Only freeze freshly caught lobster, and that means out of the water and into the freezer on the same day. Boil it first, cool it, then wrap closely in foil or heavy-gauge polythene and freeze. If preferred, split the shell in half lengthwise after cooking, remove tail and claw meat, cut into pieces, pack in a rigid container or polythene bag and freeze.

RECOMMENDED FREEZER LIFE: 1 month.

TO USE: thaw in the fridge for 6-8 hours.

## Loganberries

Choose ripe, dry fruit and only wash if absolutely necessary. Spread fruit out on trays and open-freeze. When hard, pack into polythene bags.

Less than perfect fruit can be turned into purée. Sieve the fruit and stir in sugar – about 4 oz (125 g) to 1 lb (500 g) fruit – until dissolved. Pack in rigid containers leaving ½-1 in (1-2 cm) headspace for expansion, seal and freeze.

RECOMMENDED FREEZER LIFE: 1 year.

TO USE: fruit: thaw in fridge for about 6 hours. Purée: thaw at room temperature for about 3 hours; use as required.

## Mackerel

Fish must be absolutely fresh to freeze and mackerel is no exception. A fish rich in oil, it has a delicate flavour. Gut fish, remove head, tail and fins if necessary. Wash well under running cold water, drain. Wrap each fish closely in a polythene bag, excluding as much air as possible, and freeze.

RECOMMENDED FREEZER LIFE: 2 months.

TO USE: cook from frozen.

## Mandarins

These are a small type of orange with a loose, easy-to-detach skin and sweet, juicy flesh. In season from November to January, so could be frozen during that time for use in fruit salads. Peel and remove pith, divide into segments, pack into rigid containers and cover with cold sugar syrup. Dissolve 8oz (250g) sugar in 1pt (600ml) water. Bring to boil, remove from heat and cool. Leave ½-1in (1-2cm) headspace for expansion, seal and freeze.

RECOMMENDED FREEZER LIFE: 1 year.

TO USE: thaw at room temperature for about 3 hours or overnight in fridge.

## Mangoes

These are a tropical fruit, oval in shape with a yellowish-green skin and orange-coloured flesh, tasting like a cross between peach and apricot. Freeze in sugar syrup using 8oz (250g) sugar to 1pt (600ml) water. Add 1 tbs lemon juice to each pt (600ml) of syrup. Wash, peel and slice the ripe fruit directly into the syrup. Pack in rigid containers. Put a piece of crumpled greaseproof paper on top of the fruit to keep it under the syrup, leave ½-1in (1-2cm) headspace for expansion, seal and freeze.

See *Ascorbic Acid*, for how to freeze fruit without sugar.

RECOMMENDED FREEZER LIFE: 1 year.

TO USE: thaw at room temperature for about 3 hours or overnight in the fridge.

## Margarine

This can be frozen overwrapped in foil or a polythene bag.

RECOMMENDED FREEZER LIFE: 5 months.

TO USE: thaw in fridge overnight.

## Marmalade

You don't need to freeze marmalade but you can freeze the fruit for making it. Seville oranges have a short season in the shops, so if you've no time to make marmalade when they're available, buy them to freeze and turn into marmalade when convenient. The fruit can be frozen whole or pulped. Allow one-eighth extra weight of oranges to offset the pectin loss which occurs when freezing, or add commercial liquid pectin when thawed.

*Whole fruit:* wash and dry fruit, pack into polythene bags and freeze.

*Pulp:* wash and cut up oranges, cook until reduced to a pulp. Do not add sugar. Pack into rigid containers and seal. Don't forget to make a note of the quantity of fruit pulped so you'll know how much sugar to add later. Freeze.

RECOMMENDED FREEZER LIFE: 6 months.

TO USE: whole fruit: put the frozen fruit into a pre-serving pan, cover with the required amount of water and simmer gently, covered, until fruit is soft. Then follow any standard recipe for marmalade using whole fruit method. Pulp: thaw pulp in fridge, then complete the cooking of the marmalade.

## Marrow or Squash

Young marrows can be peeled, sliced and blanched for 3 minutes, cooled, packed into polythene bags and frozen. Older marrows are best peeled, seeded, sliced and cooked until tender, then mashed, seasoned and packed into rigid containers, leaving ½-1 in (1-2 cm) headspace, sealed and frozen. They also freeze well cooked as a ragoût with tomatoes and onions.

RECOMMENDED FREEZER LIFE: blanched, 10 months; cooked, 6 months.

TO USE: heat through gently, adding a little butter.

## Marzipan

Almond paste in block form tends to crumble when thawed

and is not easy to work. It's better to freeze it already topping a cake or moulded into decorations.

RECOMMENDED FREEZER LIFE: 3 months.

TO USE: thaw marzipanned cake overnight at room temperature. Place moulded decorations on cake while frozen. They will thaw in about an hour.

## Mayonnaise

This is one of the very few non-freezers. The mixture separates on thawing and refuses to be beaten back into shape.

## Meat

*Fresh meat* stores well in the freezer but should be good-quality meat that has been hung for the correct time. Freezing won't improve quality or taste though it may tenderise it slightly.

*Cured and smoked meats* can be frozen but only for 1 month, so it's not worth preparing them specially for the freezer.

Probably your best source of supply for fresh meat is your local butcher. He can advise you on what meat to buy and when, cut it to your requirements and pack it. He may even be able to freeze it. Another source of supply is the frozen meat specialist. He will supply direct, through a frozen food wholesale shop or a cash and carry outlet. But do check what you are getting for your money. Selection packs may have a high proportion of economy cuts that you're not interested in.

If you are packing and freezing the meat yourself make sure it is well wrapped with as much air as possible excluded. Pad any bones so they don't puncture the wrappings. Chops and steaks should be open-frozen or interleaved with waxed paper before wrapping in polythene for easy separation. Meat should be rapidly frozen or it will coarsen and the subsequent loss of juices during thawing will result in a loss of flavour. So set the control of your freezer to fast-freeze 24 hours beforehand and don't freeze more than a tenth of your freezer capacity in any 24 hours. Pack the meat as close as possible to the walls to ensure rapid freezing, unless your freezer has freezing coils within the shelves.

RECOMMENDED FREEZER LIFE: beef, 8 months; lamb, 6 months; pork, 6 months.

TO USE: thaw in the fridge in wrappings, allowing 5 hours per lb (500g), or cook from frozen as follows:

*Frozen joints* should be cooked (350°F, 180°C) allowing 60 minutes per lb (500g) for lamb, 55 minutes per lb (500g) for beef, and for pork (400°F, 200°C) allowing 60 minutes per lb (500g).

*Frozen chops and steaks:* place the meat 2in (5cm) further away from the heat than usual and when almost cooked, move nearer the heat to brown.

See entries for individual meats for further details (*Bacon, Beef, Ham, Cold Meat* etc.).

## Melon

Although it loses some of its flavour and crispness in freezing, a small quantity can be usefully frozen for melon cocktails or to add to fruit salads. Choose fully ripe fruit with a good flavour, cut in half, take out seeds, then cut flesh into cubes or scoop it into balls. Mix with caster sugar – 4oz (125g) to 1lb (500g) fruit. Pack in polythene bags and freeze. Or make up a syrup using 8oz (250g) sugar to 1pt (600ml) water. Put the prepared melon into rigid containers and cover with the cold syrup. Place a piece of crumpled greaseproof paper on top of the fruit to hold it under the syrup. Leave ½-1in (1-2cm) headspace for expansion, seal and freeze.

RECOMMENDED FREEZER LIFE: 1 year.

TO USE: thaw 8 hours in fridge or at room temperature for 3 hours. It is best served while still slightly frosty.

## Meringues

These freeze beautifully. Make up meringues in the usual way. When cool pack into rigid containers and freeze. But even when frozen they are fragile, so don't put anything heavy on top of them.

RECOMMENDED FREEZER LIFE: 3 months.

TO USE: thaw about an hour at room temperature.

## Milk

Pasteurised milk doesn't freeze well because the fat separates. Homogenised milk, however, will freeze, but for a limited period – about a month. Your best plan for an emergency supply of milk would be a carton of Long Life on the shelf, which will keep for several months. If you do freeze homogenised milk don't put the bottle in the freezer as expansion in storage will cause it to crack. Pour into a waxed or polythene container allowing 1-1½in (2-3cm) headspace for expansion, seal and freeze.

RECOMMENDED FREEZER LIFE: 1 month.

TO USE: thaw in fridge overnight.

## Mince Pies

Get these made well ahead of Christmas to store in the freezer. Three-quarters of a pound (350g) of mincemeat and ½lb (250g) shortcrust pastry makes about 15 individual pies. Freeze them uncooked in patty tins. When hard, lift out of the tins, pack into rigid containers and return to freezer.

RECOMMENDED FREEZER LIFE: 3 months.

TO USE: take out number of pies you need, return them to the patty tins and bake (425°F, 220°C) for 20-30 minutes.

## Mint

Pick early in the season when full of flavour and pack whole or chopped, as mint butter or mint sauce. There's no need to blanch it, just wash and dry.

*Whole:* pack sprigs into polythene bags and freeze.

*Chopped:* chop mint finely and put into ice cube trays with a little water and freeze. Tip frozen cubes into a polythene bag, store in freezer.

*Mint butter:* cream 8oz (250g) butter, add 8tbs finely chopped mint, 1 tsp lemon juice, salt and pepper and blend well together. Shape into a roll, wrap in waxed paper, overwrap with foil and freeze.

*Mint sauce:* chop leaves finely, pack into ice cube trays, add sugar syrup just to moisten - 8oz (250g) sugar to ½pt (300ml) water. Freeze. When hard, tip cubes into polythene bag.

RECOMMENDED FREEZER LIFE: whole and chopped, 6 months; mint butter, 3 months; mint sauce, 6 months.

TO USE: crumble whole sprigs still frozen into sauces, soups or dips; thaw cubes and use as above. Mint butter: serve with lamb cutlets, peas, new potatoes. Cut off number of slices you need, re-wrap the still-frozen roll, return it to the freezer. Mint sauce: put required number of cubes into a sauceboat, thaw slightly and thin down with vinegar.

**Mushrooms**

Although these are readily available all the year, they're such a useful stand-by it's worth having some in the freezer. Button mushrooms can be frozen whole, raw or cooked, large ones should be sliced and sautéed in butter. They don't have to be blanched and, unless they are very dirty, only need a wipe with a damp cloth. Don't peel them. Spread button mushrooms on a baking tray and open-freeze.When hard, pack into a polythene bag. Slice larger ones and sauté in butter, pack in small cartons with their cooking liquid.

RECOMMENDED FREEZER LIFE: raw, 1 month; cooked, 3 months.

TO USE: from frozen in stews, soups and sauces. Whole button mushrooms can be sautéed in a little butter while frozen to serve as a vegetable.

78

## Mussels

These should be cooked before freezing. Like all shellfish, they must be very fresh for freezing. Make sure they are tightly shut; any remaining open or with broken shells should be discarded. Wash well in several changes of water, scrubbing the shells with a stiff brush, remove any fibrous matter and place in a large saucepan. Cover with a damp cloth and put over a medium heat until they open - about 3 minutes. Leave to cool, then pack with or without shells in polythene bags or rigid containers with their own juice.

RECOMMENDED FREEZER LIFE: 1 month.

TO USE: thaw overnight in the fridge in their wrappings and use as required.

## Nectarines

These are smooth-skinned peaches, smaller in size but with a richer flavour and brighter colour than ordinary peaches. Choose fruit that is soft and ripe, but not mushy, prepare and pack in sugar syrup.

Dissolve 8 oz (250 g) sugar in 1 pt (600 ml) water, bring to boil, remove from heat and leave until cold. Add ¼ tsp ascorbic acid or 1 tbs lemon juice to each pint (500 ml) of cold sugar syrup. This helps to prevent the fruit discolouring.

Skin the nectarines. If this is difficult put the fruit into boiling water for 1 minute then into cold. The skins should now rub or peel off quite easily. Slice the fruit directly into the sugar syrup in rigid containers by cutting in wedges round the stone. Discard the stone. If preferred, pack in halves. Put a piece of crumpled greaseproof paper on top of the fruit to keep it under the syrup, leave ½-1 in (1-2 cm) headspace, seal and freeze.

RECOMMENDED FREEZER LIFE: 12 months.

TO USE: thaw in fridge in container for 4-5 hours and serve while still frosty.

## Nuts

All varieties of nuts will keep fresh and moist for a year in the freezer. They can be frozen whole, chopped, flaked or toasted, but should not be salted. Pack in foil or small cartons and freeze.

RECOMMENDED FREEZER LIFE: 1 year, but only 4 months if buttered and toasted.

TO USE: thaw at room temperature for 3 hours.

For vegetarians, home-made nut butters store very well in the freezer. Cashew, pecan, walnut or filbert make a delicious change from peanut spread on wholewheat bread or toast. Put ½lb (250g) chopped nuts and 3 tbs groundnut oil in a liquidiser. Blend until smooth. Pack in small rigid container, seal and label.

RECOMMENDED FREEZER LIFE: 3 months.

TO USE: thaw at room temperature for 2-3 hours.

See entries for individual nuts for further details.

## Okra

This vegetable, also known as Lady's Fingers, is imported from tropical Africa. The edible part is the curved seed pod,

up to 9 in (23 cm) long. The pods are picked and eaten when slightly underripe. When fully ripe they are too fibrous to be digested. Because of their gluey sap they are often used in tropical cookery to thicken soups and stews.

To freeze, cut off the stems without cutting into the pod, blanch for 3 minutes (small) or 4 minutes (large), cool, drain and pack in polythene bags.

RECOMMENDED FREEZER LIFE: 1 year.

TO USE: cook from frozen in boiling water, drain and sauté in butter to serve as a vegetable, or add to stews.

## Olives

If you use olives often, the most economical way to buy them is in large jars or loose. They can be frozen but they'll keep just as well in the fridge and for the same length of time. When you have opened a jar, add a few drops of lemon juice to the brine or float lemon slices on top of the olives. This stops oxidisation. They will keep fresh this way in the jar in a fridge for 6 months.

If you want to freeze them, transfer the olives to small cartons, cover with fresh water, leave ½ in (1 cm) headspace, seal and freeze.

RECOMMENDED FREEZER LIFE: 6 months.

TO USE: thaw at room temperature and use within a day or two.

## Onions

Large onions are available all the year and can be stored easily in a dry place. So although they will freeze, it's not worth taking up too much space with them. Small pickling onions, however, are not always available and it's well worth freezing these for using whole in casseroles and sauces.

For short storage periods chopped or sliced onions need

not be blanched. For longer storage blanch them for 2
minutes, cool, drain and pack into polythene bags.
Overwrap or put in a second polythene bag to prevent
cross-flavouring with other foods. Small whole onions -
overdeveloped spring onions can be treated in the same
way - should be peeled, blanched for 3 minutes, cooled,
drained and packed in polythene bags. Again, overwrap or
put in a second polythene bag to prevent cross-flavouring.

RECOMMENDED FREEZER LIFE: unblanched, 3 months;
blanched, 6 months.

TO USE: add frozen to casseroles and sauces.

## Oranges

Buy these when cheap and freeze with sugar or in sugar
syrup. Before preparing the fruit, grate off the rind. Pack it
in small cartons or wrap in foil and freeze for later use as a
flavouring.

Remove any remaining peel, the pith and pips, and slice
the fruit, or cut into segments if preferred.

*Dry sugar:* put alternate layers of fruit and sugar into
rigid containers, using about 6 oz (175 g) sugar to 4 oranges,
seal and freeze.

*Sugar syrup:* dissolve 8 oz (250 g) sugar in 1 pt (600 ml)
water, bring to the boil, remove from heat and cool. Pack
the prepared oranges into rigid containers, cover with cold
syrup, leave ½-1 in (1-2 cm) headspace for expansion, seal
and freeze.

RECOMMENDED FREEZER LIFE: 1 year.

TO USE: grated rind: for flavouring cakes and puddings;
fruit: thaw in container about 3 hours at room temperature
and use on its own or add to fruit salads.

## Oxtail

Freeze this raw or cooked. Get the butcher to chop the oxtail
into joints. Trim off surplus fat, pack into polythene bags,
seal and freeze. Or it can be braised or made into soups.
When cold, skim fat from the surface, pack into rigid
containers, leaving ½-1 in (1-2 cm) headspace, seal and
freeze.

RECOMMENDED FREEZER LIFE: raw, 3 months; cooked, 2 months.

TO USE: raw: thaw overnight in the fridge and use as required; cooked: re-heat slowly from frozen.

## Oysters

These should be frozen the same day as they're taken from the water. Wash the outside of the shells, open them carefully retaining the juice. This is best done by holding each one over a muslin-lined strainer with a basin beneath, as you open it. Wash them in salted water, using 1 tbs salt to a pint (500 ml) cold water, drain and pack in rigid containers with the strained juices. Leave ½-1 in (1-2 cm) headspace for expansion, cover and seal.

RECOMMENDED FREEZER LIFE: 1 month.

TO USE: raw: leave in unopened container in the fridge until just thawed, 6-8 hours; cooked: add frozen to hot soup or sauce to thaw and cook at the same time. They will take about 5 minutes. Do not boil.

## Pancakes and Crêpes

Next time you're making pancakes, double the quantity you will need and freeze the surplus. Stack them one on top of the other with a piece of greaseproof paper between them. Wrap the whole pile in foil and freeze. If preferred, they can be rolled round a savoury filling and packed into foil containers ready for later baking. Cover the containers with lid or foil and freeze.

RECOMMENDED FREEZER LIFE: unfilled, 4 months; filled, 2 months.

TO USE: unfilled: unwrap, spread out and leave at room temperature about 20 minutes, then use as required. Or spread on baking tray, loosely cover with foil and re-heat for about 10 minutes (400°F, 200°C) or re-heat in a lightly greased frying pan for about ½ minute on each side. Filled: uncover container, sprinkle pancakes with grated cheese and bake from frozen (400°F, 200°C) for about 30 minutes.

## Parsley

This can be frozen whole or chopped. There's no need to blanch it first, just wash and dry the sprigs, then freeze.

*Whole:* pack sprigs of parsley into polythene bags or foil and freeze.

*Chopped:* chop finely and freeze in the little plastic containers used for individual portions of jam or pack into ice cube trays, cover with water and freeze. Tip frozen cubes into a polythene bag and store in the freezer.

RECOMMENDED FREEZER LIFE: 6 months.

TO USE: add to soups, sauces, stews, straight from the freezer. Whole sprigs can be crumbled while frozen.

## Parsnips

Choose young parsnips, scrub and trim them, peel thinly and cut into narrow strips or dice. Blanch for 2 minutes, cool, drain, spread on trays and open-freeze. When hard, pack required amounts into polythene bags and freeze.

RECOMMENDED FREEZER LIFE: 1 year.

TO USE: cook from frozen in boiling water for about 10 minutes.

## Partridge

Like all game, partridge must be hung before freezing for the same length of time as for immediate use. How long this is will depend on the weather and individual taste, but will probably be between 3 and 7 days. After this, pluck, draw and prepare in the same way as a chicken. Pack in a polythene bag, extracting as much air as possible and freeze. Pack giblets separately.

RECOMMENDED FREEZER LIFE: 6 months; giblets, 2 months.

TO USE: thaw in the fridge, allowing 5 hours per lb (500 g). Young birds are best plainly roasted, older birds can be casseroled.

## Pasta

Macaroni, spaghetti, lasagne can all be frozen most successfully. Cook pasta in the usual way - keep it slightly undercooked - drain and cool in a sieve under running cold water. Shake dry and pack in serving portions in polythene bags and freeze.

As, however, fresh pasta can be cooked in a matter of minutes it seems an unnecessary waste of freezer space. A better way to freeze pasta is as a composite dish - lasagne, layered with bolognese and cheese sauce or stuffed cannelloni with tomato or cheese sauce. If packed in foil dishes they can later be taken straight from the freezer to the oven for a quick meal.

RECOMMENDED FREEZER LIFE: cooked pasta, 1 month; composite dishes, 2-3 months.

TO USE: cooked pasta: add frozen pasta to pan of boiling water; when water returns to the boil, drain and serve. Composite dishes: remove lid or foil covering, sprinkle with grated cheese and cook (350°F, 180°C) for about 1 hour until heated through. If top seems to be drying too much, cover loosely with a piece of foil.

## Pastry

Shortcrust, puff and flaky pastry all freeze beautifully, both cooked and uncooked. In fact freezing seems to improve the flavour and texture of unbaked shortcrust. Make the pastry following any favourite recipe and freeze in quantities you are most likely to need. Flaky and puff pastry should be prepared up to the last rolling. It's best to shape the pastry into a flat oblong rather than leaving it in a lump as it will freeze and thaw faster. Wrap each piece in foil or a polythene bag, overwrap several pieces in a polythene bag, seal and freeze.

The pastry can also be shaped into flan cases or tartlet cases and frozen, baked or unbaked, uncovered in the tins. When hard, remove and pack in polythene bags and, for extra protection as they're rather fragile, stack into a box.

Pie lids can also be prepared in quantity. Cut the pastry to fit your pie dish. Stack with a piece of waxed paper between them, so that it's easy to remove one at a time. Place the pile on a piece of cardboard, wrap in foil, overwrap in a polythene bag and freeze.

RECOMMENDED FREEZER LIFE: unbaked pastry, 3 months; baked, 6 months.

TO USE: unbaked pastry and pie lids: thaw at room temperature until soft enough to roll or shape on to pie dish. Unbaked flan and tartlet cases: return to original container and bake from frozen adding about 5 minutes to normal baking time. Baked flan and tartlet cases: thaw at room temperature for about an hour and refresh in oven if liked.

## Pâté

This freezes well, but not for long as most meat or liver pâtés contain bacon which has a short freezer life. Make - and bake if necessary - your favourite pâté. When cool, cover the top with foil and freeze, or turn out of the dish, wrap in foil and freeze, or, if more practical for future use, slice and wrap each slice individually, overwrap the whole lot and freeze.

RECOMMENDED FREEZER LIFE: pâté containing bacon, 1 month; others, 3 months.

TO USE: thaw overnight in the fridge or for 6 hours at room temperature.

FOODS

## Peaches

Fully ripe peaches with a good flavour are the ones to freeze. If possible taste one before buying a quantity. Often the flavour of a peach doesn't measure up to its looks. Prepare and pack them in sugar syrup and, as they discolour quickly when exposed to the air, have the syrup ready so the fruit can be dropped straight into it.

Dissolve 8 oz (250 g) sugar in 1 pint (600 ml) water, bring to the boil, remove from heat and leave until cold. Add ¼ tsp ascorbic acid or 1 tbs lemon juice to each pint (600 ml) of cold sugar syrup. This helps to prevent the fruit discolouring.

Peel the peaches. If this is difficult, put the fruit into boiling water for 1 minute, then into cold. The skins should now rub or peel off quite easily. Slice the fruit directly into the sugar syrup in rigid containers by cutting in wedges round the stone. Discard the stone. If preferred, pack in halves. Put a piece of crumpled greaseproof paper on top of the fruit to keep it under the syrup, leave ½-1 in (1-2 cm) headspace, seal and freeze.

See *Ascorbic Acid* for how to freeze fruit without sugar.

RECOMMENDED FREEZER LIFE: 1 year.

TO USE: thaw in container for 3-4 hours at room temperature and serve while still frosty.

## Pears

The best way to freeze pears is lightly cooked. They lose their delicate flavour and crisp texture when frozen raw. Choose firm, just ripe pears. Skin, halve and core them, then poach for 1½ minutes in sugar syrup - 8 oz (250 g) sugar to 1 pint (600 ml) water. Add a vanilla pod to the syrup for extra flavour. Or poach them in honey and water - a dessertspoon of honey to a cup of water. Commice pears done this way are particularly good. Leave until cold, pack into rigid containers with the poaching syrup, top with a piece of crumpled greaseproof paper, leave ½-1 in (1-2 cm) headspace, seal and freeze.

RECOMMENDED FREEZER LIFE: 1 year.

TO USE: thaw in container for 3-4 hours at room temperature.

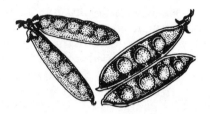

## Peas

Pick them while they are still young and sweet. Pod them as soon as they have been gathered and blanch for 1 minute, cool and drain. Open-freeze on trays until hard, then pack into a polythene bag and return to the freezer or pack in required amounts in polythene bags, seal and freeze.

*Mange-tout:* these should be picked when the pod is flat. If the peas have begun to swell the pods will be stringy round the outside. Top and tail, string them and blanch for 2 minutes, cool, drain and freeze as above.

RECOMMENDED FREEZER LIFE: 1 year.

TO USE: cook from frozen in boiling water for about 5 minutes.

## Peppers

Whether you choose red, green or yellow sweet peppers to freeze, make sure they are firm with glossy skins. Wash or wipe them, cut off the stems and remove all seeds and membrane. Cut in halves, slices or rings. Blanch - halves for 3 minutes, slices or rings for 2 minutes - cool, drain and pack in polythene bags.

For short-term storage they may be frozen unblanched.

RECOMMENDED FREEZER LIFE: blanched, 1 year; unblanched, 3 months.

TO USE: add to stews and casseroles from frozen or thaw and use as required.

## Persimmons

Also known as date plums these are of Japanese origin but are now cultivated commercially in a number of countries. The fruit is the size of a large tomato, and yellow to red in colour. It should be soft and ripe for freezing. Wash and dry it, remove stem ends, peel and freeze whole in sugar syrup. Pack fruit into rigid containers and cover with cold sugar syrup - 8oz (250g) sugar to 1 pint (600ml) water and 1 tbs lemon juice. Leave ½-1in (1-2cm) headspace, seal and freeze.

RECOMMENDED FREEZER LIFE: 1 year.

TO USE: thaw in container for 3-4 hours at room temperature.

## Pheasant

One of the finest game birds for roasting. Hen birds are generally considered more succulent than the cocks. Like all game it needs to be well hung if the flesh is to be tender and well flavoured. The time it takes will depend on the weather and your own taste. It could be a week or even two, but the birds should smell 'gamey' and the flesh on the breast should have begun to change colour. At this stage, pluck, draw and prepare in the same way as a chicken. Pack in a polythene bag, extracting as much air as possible, and freeze.

RECOMMENDED FREEZER LIFE: 6 months.

TO USE: thaw in the fridge allowing 5 hours per lb (500g). Young birds are best plainly roasted, older birds can be casseroled or made into pies or pâtés.

## Pies

These freeze well unbaked or baked. Make large or small pies in foil dishes, double-crusted ones in patty tins. If freezing unbaked do not make a steam vent. Open-freeze and when hard, leave pies in foil dishes and seal with foil. Remove small pies from patty tins and pack in foil or polythene bags.

If freezing baked, remember to underbake slightly as they will brown more when re-heated. Cool quickly, pack in foil and freeze.

When making double-crust fruit pies it's a good idea to add a little cornflour to the sugar to help thicken the juices and so prevent a soggy bottom crust. Use 1 tsp cornflour to 2 tbs sugar and toss the fruit in this before putting it on to the pastry. Or you can brush the inside of the case with a little beaten egg white before putting in the filling.

RECOMMENDED FREEZER LIFE: unbaked, 3 months; baked, meat pies, 3-4 months; fruit pies, up to 6 months.

TO USE: unbaked: unwrap and place in pre-heated oven and bake as usual, allowing extra time for thawing. Cut a vent in the pastry when it begins to thaw. Baked: leave at room temperature for 2-4 hours depending on size of pie, then re-heat (350°F, 180°C).

## Pigeon

Pluck and draw before freezing and truss in the same way as chickens. Pad bones with a piece of foil and pack in polythene bags, excluding as much air as possible, seal and freeze.

They can also be casseroled or made into pâté and frozen in this way.

RECOMMENDED FREEZER LIFE: 6 months; casseroled, 4 months; pâté, 4 weeks.

TO USE: raw: thaw in fridge allowing 5 hours per lb (500 g). Casseroled: heat from frozen in a slow oven. Pâté: thaw in fridge overnight.

## Pimentoes

Another name for *Peppers*.

## Pineapple

These can often be bought quite cheaply in the summer and freeze very well with sugar or in sugar syrup. Choose ripe fruit (one of the inner leaves of the crown should pull out easily if it is), peel, remove eyes and core and slice or dice. Mix with sugar - 4oz (125g) to 1lb (500g) fruit, pack in polythene bags, seal and freeze. Or pack pieces into rigid containers and cover with cold sugar syrup - 8oz (250g) sugar dissolved in 1pt (600ml) water - cover fruit with crumpled greaseproof paper, leave ½-1in (1-2cm) head-space, seal and freeze.

RECOMMENDED FREEZER LIFE: 1 year.

TO USE: thaw in container for 3-4 hours at room temperature.

## Pizza

These are useful for snack meals or to serve with drinks. Bought ones can be frozen or if you're a bread maker use a batch of dough to make your own pizza. The classic topping is tomatoes, cheese, anchovy fillets and basil, but you can devise any savoury combination - mushroom, ham, tomatoes, cheese, tomatoes - to suit yourself. When baked, cool and open-freeze, then wrap each one in foil, overwrap them all in a polythene bag and return to the freezer.

RECOMMENDED FREEZER LIFE: 3 months.

TO USE: heat from frozen (400°F, 200°C) for about 35 minutes or thaw 2 hours at room temperature and heat through at above temperature for 15 minutes.

## Plums

Choose firm, ripe fruit with no blemishes. Wash if necessary and dry. They can be frozen whole as a dry pack, but the skins tend to toughen and the stones flavour the fruit during long-term storage, so this method is not recommended except for short periods of up to 3 months. The most successful ways of freezing them are:

1. Halve, stone and pack in rigid containers with cold syrup. Put a piece of crumpled greaseproof paper on top of the fruit to keep it under the syrup. Leave ½-1in (1-2cm) headspace for expansion, seal and freeze.

2. Halve, stone and stew the fruit. Pack in rigid

containers, leaving ½-1in (1-2cm) headspace, seal and freeze.

RECOMMENDED FREEZER LIFE: 1 year.

TO USE: fruit in syrup can be cooked from frozen; stewed fruit should be thawed at room temperature for 2-4 hours.

## Pomegranate

This is a fruit the size of an orange with a hard thick russet-coloured skin and red flesh containing numerous seeds. Cut the ripe fruit in half, scoop out the juice sacs, pack the fruit into rigid containers and cover with sugar syrup – 8oz (250g) sugar dissolved in 1pt (600ml) water. Leave ½-1in (1-2cm) headspace, seal and freeze.

RECOMMENDED FREEZER LIFE: 1 year.

TO USE: thaw in containers for 2-4 hours at room temperature.

## Pork

Unless you're a great pork-eating family you won't want to invest in a whole pig for the freezer. For one thing you'll find yourself with a number of cuts you're perhaps unlikely to use, including the head and trotters, and for another, pork has a shorter freezer life (6 months) than other meat because of its fatty composition, so you won't want to buy more than you can use up within this time limit.

Better to buy only the cuts you regularly use and enjoy, and freeze those. Look for pork with firm, pinkish, lean meat and creamy white fat. If you like crackling see that the skin is deeply and evenly scored.

When packing it for the freezer, trim off surplus fat, pad any bones so they don't puncture the wrappings and wrap tightly in foil or polythene bags. Chops should be open-frozen or interleaved with waxed paper before wrapping in polythene for easy separation. Pack the meat as closely as possible to the walls to ensure rapid freezing.

RECOMMENDED FREEZER LIFE: 6 months.

TO USE: thaw in the fridge in wrappings, allowing 5 hours per lb (500g) or cook from frozen (350°F, 180°C) allowing 60 minutes per lb (500g). Frozen chops should be placed 2 in

(5cm) further from heat than usual and when almost cooked moved nearer to the heat to brown.

## Potatoes

These can be cooked in a variety of ways and frozen.

*Baked:* it's not worth baking them specially to freeze but if you have left-over jacket potatoes, cut them in half, scoop out the cooked potato, mash it with a little butter and seasoning or grated cheese, replace in shells, cover with foil and freeze.

RECOMMENDED FREEZER LIFE: 3 months.

TO USE: place, still wrapped in foil in the oven (400°F, 200°C) for about 30 minutes, unwrap, sprinkle cut surface with grated cheese, return to oven to brown.

*Chips:* commercially frozen chips can be bought in bulk packages and are very good. If you are making your own, prepare potatoes and fry gently in clean fat until just soft but not coloured. Lift out and drain on absorbent paper, cool, open-freeze and pack in polythene bags.

RECOMMENDED FREEZER LIFE: 6 months.

TO USE: deep-fry from frozen to a deep golden brown. Take care to use a basket and fairly deep chip pan and cook only a few at a time. The frozen chips will cause spitting. Lift the basket in and out frequently to start with or the fat could boil over.

*Croquettes:* boil potatoes, mash with a little milk, season, beat in one egg to every lb (500 g) of mashed potato. Divide into small portions, roll into cork shapes, brush with beaten egg and coat with browned breadcrumbs. Open-freeze and when hard, pack into polythene bags.

RECOMMENDED FREEZER LIFE: 3 months.

TO USE: thaw and fry in deep fat for about 4 minutes, or

bake from frozen (375°F, 190°C) for about 15 minutes.

*New boiled:* slightly undercook with a little mint, toss in butter, cool and pack in polythene bags or freezer-cooking bags.

RECOMMENDED FREEZER LIFE: 3 months.

TO USE: thaw and re-heat in the melted butter or put freezer-cooking bag into boiling water, remove from heat and leave for 10 minutes.

*Roast:* roast potatoes in usual way, drain well on absorbent paper and cool. Pack in polythene bags, seal and freeze.

RECOMMENDED FREEZER LIFE: 3 months.

TO USE: put the frozen potatoes in a roasting tin containing a very little hot oil, turn them in the oil and re-heat in the oven (400°F, 200°C) for 30 minutes.


## Prawns

As with all shellfish, these must be absolutely fresh for freezing. Wash thoroughly. Boil in lightly salted water until they turn pink - 2-4 minutes; cool in the liquid. Shell and pack tightly in polythene bags, seal and freeze. If you haven't time to cook and prepare them they can be frozen raw. Simply remove the heads, wash in salted water, drain and pack into polythene bags, seal and freeze.

RECOMMENDED FREEZER LIFE: 1 month.

TO USE: cooked: thaw prawns in the fridge for use in salads; add to cooked dishes while still frozen. Raw: drop into boiling, lightly salted water and when the water returns to the boil, simmer for 2-4 minutes.


## Puddings and Desserts

If you're a pudding-eating family you'll find it a time- and energy-saver to cook one, freeze one.

*Steamed puddings:* both suet and sponge mixtures can be made and cooked in the usual way - in foil basins if possible - then cooled, wrapped and frozen. Add dried fruits to the mixture or coffee or chocolate flavourings, but don't put jam or syrup in the bottom as the puddings tend to become soggy when thawing.

RECOMMENDED FREEZER LIFE: 3 months.

TO USE: re-heat from frozen by boiling for about an hour or until heated through.

*Baked puddings:* a sponge mixture can also be baked as a cake, cooled and frozen for later use with whipped cream and fruit. It can be made into an upside-down pudding, baked, turned out and when cold, open-frozen. When hard it should be wrapped in foil and returned to the freezer.

RECOMMENDED FREEZER LIFE: 3 months.

TO USE: thaw at room temperature 3-4 hours and serve cold, or thaw at room temperature for 2 hours and then heat (375°F, 190°C) for 30 minutes.

*Fruit crumble:* make as usual and freeze raw or freeze the crumble mixture separately.

RECOMMENDED FREEZER LIFE: 3 months.

TO USE: bake from frozen (375°F, 190°C) about 1 hour, or sprinkle frozen crumble over fresh fruit and bake as usual.

*Fruit pies:* use foil pie dishes and make in the usual way. Freeze raw or cooked.

RECOMMENDED FREEZER LIFE: 3 months.

TO USE: raw: cook from frozen (400°F, 200°C) for 1 hour. Cooked: re-heat (375°F, 190°C) for 30-40 minutes.

*Milk puddings:* rice pudding, which takes a long time to cook, can be frozen, but semolina is not really worth freezing as it doesn't take any longer to cook from fresh than to thaw and re-heat.

RECOMMENDED FREEZER LIFE: 3 months.

TO USE: add a little milk and re-heat in a pan over a low heat.

*Cold puddings:* mousses and cold soufflés freeze well, but not clear fruit jellies; they tend to go granular and rubbery.

RECOMMENDED FREEZER LIFE: 3 months.

TO USE: thaw in the fridge about 2 hours.

See also *Christmas Pudding.*

## Pulses

Because they need fairly lengthy soaking and cooking, pulses - dried beans, peas and lentils - are not made as much use of as they might be. Freezer owners, however, can soak and cook them in quantity, then freeze them away for future use in soups, stews or as a nourishing and filling vegetable. Buy them from a health food store or a grocer with a quick turnover; you don't want them old and tired. Soak and cook them in the usual way, keeping them slightly undercooked. Drain, cool, pat dry and freeze in rigid containers.

RECOMMENDED FREEZER LIFE: 6 months.

TO USE: thaw, purée and blend with stock for soup; add to stews in time to finish cooking them. To serve as a vegetable heat in the top of a double boiler with a lump of butter.

## Pumpkin

Wash pumpkin, peel and cut in half, remove seeds and strings, cut into slices or cubes. Steam or boil until tender. Mash. Cool and pack into rigid containers, leaving ½-1 in (1-2cm) headspace and freeze.

RECOMMENDED FREEZER LIFE: 1 year.

TO USE: thaw in the top of a double boiler, season and serve as a vegetable or thaw in the fridge and use to make a pumpkin pie. Or pumpkin soup: sieve or blend in liquidiser 2oz (50g) lightly fried onion with mashed pumpkin. Add 1pt (500ml) chicken stock, ¼pt (125ml) cream, stir well and re-heat gently. Serve with fried croûtons.

**Purée, Fruit**. See *Apples, Strawberries* etc.

## Quail

Pluck and singe, but do not draw as they are eaten whole. Cut off head and neck and take out the crop. Pack in polythene bags or, if more convenient as 1 bird per person is needed, in twos or fours in foil trays, overwrapped in polythene bags, seal and freeze.

RECOMMENDED FREEZER LIFE: 6 months.

TO USE: thaw in the fridge, allowing 5 hours per lb (500 g) before roasting.

## Quiches

These savoury flans are marvellous for suppers and snacks, picnics and parties. Well worth some freezer space, they are best baked before being frozen. Use any savoury filling – bacon, onion and cheese; ham and sweetcorn; mushroom; shellfish. When baked, open-freeze and when hard, remove from flan tin, wrap in foil, overwrap in a polythene bag, seal and freeze.

RECOMMENDED FREEZER LIFE: 2 months.

TO USE: loosen wrappings and thaw at room temperature for 2 hours to serve cold, or heat through (350°F, 180°C) about 20 minutes.

## Quince

This fruit with its hard, sour flesh has a yellowish or russet-coloured skin with a soft down on it when ripe. When cooked with sugar it turns a dull pink colour and makes a delicious jelly or preserve. It can also be cooked with apples or pears to give added flavour. For this purpose it can be frozen. Peel, quarter and core the fruit, removing any hard pieces round the core. Cut it into chunks, blanch for 2 minutes, cool, drain and open-freeze on trays, and when hard pack into a polythene bag, or freeze in small quantities in polythene bags.

RECOMMENDED FREEZER LIFE: 1 year.

TO USE: stew gently with a little sugar and enough water to prevent them burning until tender, then add to apple pies or puddings or pear dishes.

## Rabbit

Rabbit should be frozen when absolutely fresh. Skin and draw the rabbit and wipe over the inside with a damp cloth. Cut it into joints, pack in polythene bags and freeze.

RECOMMENDED FREEZER LIFE: 6 months.

TO USE: thaw in wrapping in the fridge, allowing 5 hours per lb (500g). If the rabbit is very young it can be roasted, otherwise it can be braised, fricasséed or made into a pie.

## Raspberries

Probably the most successful fruit to freeze. They retain their colour and flavour from one season to the next. If anything, freezing seems to intensify the flavour. They can be frozen with or without sugar or as a purée.

Pick over the fruit, discarding any hulls or hard berries – damaged ones can be turned into purée. Do not wash. Spread out on trays and open-freeze. When hard pack into polythene bags, seal and return to the freezer.

If preferred, pack with sugar. Allow 4oz (125g) sugar to 1lb (500g) fruit, mix gently together and pack in poly-thene bags in ½lb or 1 lb (250 or 500g) quantities, seal and freeze.

*Purée:* sieve the fruit and stir in sugar to taste – about 4 oz (125 g) sugar to 1 lb (500 g) fruit. When sugar has dissolved, pour the purée into rigid containers, leave ½-1 in (1-2 cm) headspace, seal and freeze.

RECOMMENDED FREEZER LIFE: 1 year.

TO USE: thaw at room temperature for about 3 hours. The thawing of purée can be speeded up by standing the sealed container in a pan of water. Use it as a sauce with puddings or meringues and cream or make it into a mousse, soufflé or ice cream. Open-frozen fruit can be used to decorate puddings.

## Redcurrants

Strip the fruit off the stalks, wash if necessary and dry. Spread out on trays and open-freeze. When hard pack into polythene bags, seal and return to the freezer. If preferred, they can be frozen with sugar – 4 oz (125 g) to 1 lb (500 g) fruit. Mix the two together, then pack into polythene bags and freeze.

RECOMMENDED FREEZER LIFE: 1 year.

TO USE: thaw about 3 hours at room temperature or cook from frozen. Open-frozen fruit can be used for decorating puddings.

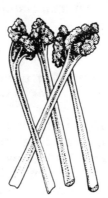

## Rhubarb

Pick the fruit early in the season while the sticks are young and tender. Wash, trim and cut into 1-in (2-cm) lengths. Blanch for 1 minute, cool quickly and pack into polythene bags. Rhubarb can be frozen raw but it takes up more room and the colour is not so good. It can also be stewed, sweetened and sieved and frozen as a purée in rigid containers. Leave ½-1 in (1-2 cm) headspace for expansion, seal and freeze.

RECOMMENDED FREEZER LIFE: 1 year.

TO USE: put frozen rhubarb in a pan with just enough water to prevent sticking and about 4 oz (125 g) sugar to 1 lb (500 g) fruit. Heat gently until cooked. For pies and tarts, partially thaw before using. Thaw the purée at room temperature for about 3 hours.

## Rice

This freezes well but takes as long to thaw and re-heat as to cook from raw, so there seems little point in taking up valuable freezer space with it. If, however, you have left-over cooked rice, freeze it for later use in stuffed tomatoes, peppers or to add to soup. Pack the rice loosely in a polythene bag, seal and place in the freezer. When it is half frozen, squeeze the bag with both hands to separate the grains. Replace in the freezer.

RECOMMENDED FREEZER LIFE: 6 months.

TO USE: frozen rice can be added to hot soup which should then be brought back to the boil. To use as a stuffing ingredient thaw at room temperature for about an hour then use as required.

## Risotto

This too can be frozen either quite plain or with the addition of chicken, mushrooms, prawns, chicken livers or peas.

For a plain risotto, chop an onion finely, soften it in a little butter, stir in 8 oz (250g) rice. When it looks transparent pour in a glass of white wine, let it bubble until it has almost disappeared then add about ½ pt (300 ml) chicken stock. When it has been absorbed add more – you will need about 1½ pts – (1 l) – and continue cooking until the rice is soft and moist. It will take about 20 minutes. Stir continuously towards the end of the cooking time or it will stick. Stir in an ounce (30g) each of butter and grated cheese, cool and pack in rigid containers.

RECOMMENDED FREEZER LIFE: 2 months.

TO USE: thaw overnight in the fridge then re-heat gently in the top of a double boiler, adjusting the seasoning.

## Rum Babas

These individual cakes or puddings are made from a yeast dough enriched with eggs and sugar. It's probably easier to freeze them before soaking them in syrup. Pack the baked and cooled rum babas into polythene bags; seal and freeze.

RECOMMENDED FREEZER LIFE: 3 months.

TO USE: unpack and stand the babas on a cake rack for about 45 minutes. Make holes all over the top and sides with a fine skewer. Stand them in a dish or deep serving plate and pour over a hot rum-flavoured syrup. Baste them well so they are really moist. Serve with whipped cream. Add 1 tbs rum to the cream as you whip for a specially rich effect. Decorate with glacé cherries and angelica if liked.

**Runner Beans.** See *Beans, Runner.*

# S

## Sage

Just wash, dry and chop the leaves – no need to blanch – then pack into the little plastic containers used for individual portions of jam or pack into ice cube trays, cover with water and freeze. Tip frozen cubes into a polythene bag and store in the freezer.

RECOMMENDED FREEZER LIFE: 6 months.

TO USE: thaw and add to stuffings and pork dishes.

## Salad Vegetables

Lettuce, tomatoes, watercress, cucumbers and spring onions are no good for eating raw after freezing. They become wet and mushy.

## Salmon

As with all fish, salmon must be absolutely fresh to freeze at home, ideally caught and frozen on the same day.

Scale the fish, gut it, wash thoroughly under running cold water, drain and dry. It can be left whole or cut into two or three joints, or the head and tail removed, then cut across the bone into 1-in (2-cm) steaks. Wrap in heavy-gauge polythene and freeze.

If you want to freeze it whole it should not be more than 2 in (5 cm) thick. To protect the fish from the drying effects of the freezer it is a good idea to ice-glaze it. To do this place the unwrapped fish in the freezer and leave until hard. Remove, dip in cold fresh water. A thin film of ice will form over the fish. Return it to the freezer. Repeat about three times at half-hourly intervals. Wrap in heavy-gauge polythene and return to the freezer

RECOMMENDED FREEZER LIFE: 2 months.

TO USE: thaw whole fish and large joints slowly in wrappings in cool place. A whole salmon will take up to 24 hours. Salmon steaks can be cooked from frozen.

## Salsify

Also known as the vegetable oyster because of its delicate oyster-like flavour. Use the roots when young and tender. Scrub them, do not peel, blanch for 2 minutes. Cut into 2-3-in (5-6-cm) lengths and peel while still warm. Leave to cool then pack in polythene bags and freeze.

RECOMMENDED FREEZER LIFE: 1 year.

TO USE: cook from frozen in boiling water and serve in a white sauce or tossed in melted butter.

## Sandwiches

If you always seem to be making sandwiches for picnics, parties, packed lunches, plan a sandwich-making session and prepare several different kinds to freeze, and then draw on them over a period of weeks.

Use day-old bread, soften the butter or margarine and spread it right to the edge of the bread to prevent the filling soaking in. Fill the sandwiches, stack them and cut with a sharp knife. Don't wrap more than six or eight sandwiches together. And if you want to make up a packet of mixed fillings, wrap each flavour separately, then overwrap the whole lot in foil or a polythene bag and freeze.

A wide range of fillings can be used – cheese, fish, meat, pâté – in any number of combinations. But avoid hard-boiled eggs which go rubbery, mayonnaise which curdles, salad vegetables which go limp, and jam which makes the bread soggy on thawing.

Open sandwiches can be frozen unwrapped on trays, then packed in rigid containers with freezer paper between the layers. When needed, arrange on a serving dish while frozen and leave to thaw.

Pinwheel and ribbon sandwiches should be frozen uncut. When needed, partially thaw, slice, arrange on a serving plate, cover and finish thawing.

RECOMMENDED FREEZER LIFE: 2 months.

TO USE: thaw in wrappings at room temperature for about 3 hours.

## Sauces

Freeze away some containers of white, brown and tomato sauces and you'll have the basis for almost all the dishes – simple and advanced – that you're likely to need. They're no more trouble to make in bulk, so make up 2 or even 4 pts (1 or 2 litres) and freeze in ½ pt (250 ml) quantities to use on their own or as a basis for many others.

A ½ pt (250 ml) basic white sauce when thawed can be turned into:

*Mushroom sauce* by the addition of 3 oz (75 g) sautéed mushrooms plus seasonings.

*Cheese sauce* by the addition of 2 oz (50 g) grated cheese and ½ tsp made mustard. (See also entry under *Cheese Sauce.*)

*Onion sauce* by the addition of a large onion, chopped, sautéed in butter until soft, then puréed. Add extra seasoning.

*Shrimp sauce* by the addition of 2 oz (50 g) shrimps and a squeeze of lemon juice.

In the same way a basic brown or espagnole sauce can quickly be turned into a number of other exciting sauces.

*Tomato sauce* can be used to enliven meat, vegetable and pasta dishes or as the basis of a barbecue sauce.

And don't forget those sauces complete in themselves: meat sauce, curry sauce, bread sauce and apple sauce. They all freeze well and are great time-savers when it comes to producing a meal.

Pack the sauces in rigid containers, leaving ½-1 in (1-2 cm) headspace, seal and freeze.

RECOMMENDED FREEZER LIFE: white and brown sauces, 6 months; tomato sauce, 1 year; meat, curry and bread sauces, 3 months; apple sauce, 1 year.

TO USE: apple sauce: thaw at room temperature. White sauce can usually be restored to its original consistency if re-heated slowly in a thick pan or double boiler and beaten well with a wooden spoon. Alternatively, if you don't mind the rather gelatinous consistency, you can substitute cornflour for wheat flour; you will only need half as much cornflour as wheat flour. The rest of the sauces: thaw gently in double boiler or non-stick thick pan, adjust seasoning.

## Sausages

Freshly made sausages and sausage meat bought from the butcher may be frozen. Pack in polythene bags in ½ or 1 lb (250 or 500 g) quantities, seal and freeze. If you are making your own sausages for freezing, don't season them too highly.

RECOMMENDED FREEZER LIFE: 6 months.

TO USE: sausages: thaw in the fridge and fry, or partially thaw to separate and fry gently, or cook in a moderate oven. Sausage meat: thaw in the fridge and use as required.

## Sausage Rolls

These can be made with shortcrust or puff pastry and frozen unbaked or baked. Open-freeze unbaked sausage rolls and when hard, pack them into polythene bags or rigid containers. Pack baked sausage rolls in rigid containers with foil or freezer paper between the layers.

RECOMMENDED FREEZER LIFE: 3 months.

TO USE: unbaked: arrange on a baking sheet, brush with beaten egg and bake from frozen (425°F, 220°C) for about 30 minutes. Baked: thaw in the fridge and then refresh in a moderate oven.

## Savarin

This is made from the same basic yeast mixture as rum babas but baked in a large ring mould. Freeze, thaw and finish as for rum babas. If liked the centre can be filled with fruit, and cream served separately.

## Scallops

These should be frozen the same day as they're taken from the water. Scrub the outside of the shells thoroughly. Place them in a hot oven for a few minutes and remove as soon as the shells open. Take off the black fringe round the scallop. Wash the fish in salted water. Cut it away from the shell with its orange roe, rinse and drain. Pack into rigid containers, cover and freeze. They can also be frozen as a cooked dish.

RECOMMENDED FREEZER LIFE: 1 month.

TO USE: thaw in the fridge overnight and use as fresh scallops, or put from frozen into hot water or sauce to thaw and cook. Re-heat cooked dish from frozen.

## Scampi

As with all shellfish these must be absolutely fresh and give the best results when frozen raw. Twist off the head and carapace with legs and claws attached. Wash the tails and pack tightly into rigid containers or polythene bags and freeze.

RECOMMENDED FREEZER LIFE: 1 month.

TO USE: put small quantities of the frozen tails into boiling salted water and when the water returns to the boil simmer for 4-6 minutes depending on size. Cool and serve.

## Scones

These don't keep fresh long after baking, even kept in tins, but they do freeze very well. Pack the cooked, cooled scones in polythene bags, seal and freeze.

RECOMMENDED FREEZER LIFE: 6 months.

TO USE: thaw in wrappings at room temperature for about an hour or spread on a baking tray, cover with foil and re-heat in the oven (400°F, 200°C) for 10 minutes.

## Scorzonera

This is the black-rooted variety of salsify and considered to have a finer flavour. Prepare, freeze and use as for salsify, q.v.

## Swiss Chard

This is a form of beet grown for its leaves. The thick mid-ribs are cooked like celery and the glossy leaves as spinach. Pick regularly to keep the plants productive, twisting a few of the outer leaves from the base of each plant. Strip off the green part of the leaf, blanch for 2 minutes, cool, drain and pack into polythene bags, seal and freeze. Cut the mid-ribs into 2-in (5-cm) sticks and blanch for 3 minutes, cool, drain and pack into polythene bags or rigid containers, seal and freeze.

RECOMMENDED FREEZER LIFE: 1 year.

TO USE: cook from frozen in boiling water.

## Shallots

Like onions, of which family they are the mild member, shallots store well, but if it's more convenient to have them prepared and frozen, then this can be done. They can be left whole or chopped. Peel and blanch whole shallots for 2 minutes or chop and blanch them for 1 minute. Cool, drain and open-freeze, then pack into polythene bags. Overwrap them so their smell isn't absorbed by other foods in the freezer.

RECOMMENDED FREEZER LIFE: 6 months.

TO USE: add frozen to stews, casseroles and sauces.

## Shellfish

If you have access to freshly caught shellfish then it can be frozen at home, but it must be absolutely fresh. See under *Crab, Lobster* etc. for ways of preparing and freezing it.

RECOMMENDED FREEZER LIFE: 1 month.

## Shortbread

This stores well in an airtight tin for a week or two, but will keep much longer in the freezer and emerge as fresh and crisp as the day it was baked. Make and bake in the usual way, cool and wrap in foil.

RECOMMENDED FREEZER LIFE: 3 months.

TO USE: thaw at room temperature about 4 hours.

107

## Shrimps

These must be absolutely fresh for freezing. Wash
thoroughly in fresh cold water. Boil in lightly salted water
until they turn pink – 2-4 minutes – cool in the liquid.
Shell and pack in polythene bags, seal and freeze. If you
haven't time to cook and prepare them they can be frozen
raw. Simply remove the heads, wash in salted water, drain
and pack into polythene bags, seal and freeze.

RECOMMENDED FREEZER LIFE: raw, cooked or potted, 1
month.

TO USE: raw: drop into boiling, lightly salted water and
when the water returns to the boil, simmer for 2-4 minutes.
Cooked: thaw shrimps in the fridge for use in salads and
cold dishes; add them, still frozen, to cooked dishes just
before end of cooking time to heat through.

## Smoked Haddock. See *Haddock*.

## Sole

This can be frozen if it is really fresh. Skin, scale and gut it,
wash thoroughly in cold water, drain and dry. The fish can
be frozen on the bone or in fillets. Wrap closely in
polythene bags, excluding as much air as possible, seal and
freeze.

RECOMMENDED FREEZER LIFE: 3 months.

TO USE: cook from frozen but if thawing is preferred or
necessary, allow 5 hours per pound (500 g) in the fridge.

## Sorbets

These are light and refreshing ices simply made by freezing
together fruit juice or purée, sugar syrup and beaten egg
white. They are really best when freshly made. With a stock
of fruit purées (apricot, raspberry, blackcurrant) and juices
(orange, lemon, pineapple) kept in your freezer you can
make them as you need them. Combine ½ pt (250 ml) water
with 3 oz (75 g) sugar and boil for 5 minutes to make syrup.

Stir in ½pt (250ml) purée or juice. Cool and freeze until just solid. Fold in a stiffly whisked egg white and return to freezer.

RECOMMENDED FREEZER LIFE: 2 months.

TO USE: thaw at room temperature about 10 minutes.

## Soufflés

Sweet or savoury soufflés, both those to be served cold and those to be served hot, freeze extremely well. Prepare the soufflé dish (make sure it is one that will stand the low temperature of the freezer) in the usual way, but use foil rather than greaseproof paper to form the collar 1-2 in (3-4cm) above the rim of the dish. Secure it firmly with freezer tape. Pour soufflé mixture into the prepared dish. Do not decorate at this stage. Open-freeze by standing on a flat tray in the freezer until hard. Remove from tray, place soufflé dish with collar still in position in a polythene bag, seal and return to the freezer.

You can use individual ramekins instead of one large soufflé dish.

RECOMMENDED FREEZER LIFE: 2 months.

TO USE: cold soufflés: remove polythene bag, but not the collar, and thaw overnight in the fridge or at room temperature for about 4 hours. When thawed, carefully remove collar and decorate soufflé.

Hot soufflés: thaw small soufflés 20 minutes at room temperature, large ones 30 minutes. Bake at 375°F, 190°C for 25-30 minutes if in ramekins, 70 minutes if in one large dish, until risen and golden. Serve as usual.

## Soup

Any favourite soup can be prepared in double or treble quantities and the surplus frozen. Cool and skim off excess fat before freezing. It is best to add milk or cream to soups after thawing. Pour into rigid containers leaving ½-1 in (1-2cm) headspace, seal and freeze.

RECOMMENDED FREEZER LIFE: 3 months.

TO USE: hold sealed container under running hot water for a moment until contents loosen. Re-heat in a saucepan, using a low heat until thawed. Do not boil. Adjust the seasoning before serving.

**Spaghetti.** See *Pasta.*

### Spices

After 3-4 months spices seem to change their flavour, becoming peppery or fading. So to retain their true flavour it's best not to leave spiced dishes in the freezer longer than 2 months.

### Spinach

As you can blanch only a small quantity of leaves at a time, it's a long job to prepare a large batch for the freezer. It's far simpler and just as good to cook it, then freeze it.

Strip the leaves off the stalks, wash thoroughly and put in a large saucepan – don't add any more water, there's enough clinging to the leaves. Cook until tender, drain, cool and then squeeze or press out excess moisture. Chop and pack into polythene bags in small quantities, seal and freeze.

RECOMMENDED FREEZER LIFE: 1 year.

TO USE: re-heat gently from frozen in a thick saucepan, stirring occasionally. Season and add a little butter and/or cream.

### Sponge Cakes

These freeze beautifully and are useful to have in the freezer for use with fruit and cream as a pudding, or with jam, cream or butter icing as a cake. They can be butter-iced before freezing, in which case open-freeze them until hard and then pack into a polythene bag or rigid container so that the icing won't get damaged. Don't fill with jam or fruit before freezing, as the cakes go soggy when thawed. Just wrap the sponge layers separately or slip a piece of waxed or greaseproof paper between the layers before packing into a polythene bag or rigid container. It's only a matter of moments to fill them when thawed.

RECOMMENDED FREEZER LIFE: plain, 4 months; with buttercream, 3 months.

TO USE: thaw about 2 hours at room temperature; if butter-iced remove wrappings before thawing so that they don't stick to the surface and spoil the icing.

**Sponge Puddings:** See under *Puddings and Desserts*.

### Steak

Grilling or frying steaks should be cut into one-portion pieces. Open-freeze, wrap each steak flat in polythene or interleave the steaks with a piece of waxed or freezer paper. Pack 2 or 3 together in a polythene bag. Seal and place in the coldest part of the freezer so they will freeze rapidly.

RECOMMENDED FREEZER LIFE: 6 months.

TO USE: thaw in the fridge in their wrappings or cook from frozen. To grill frozen steak, place it 2 in (5 cm) further away from the heat than usual until nearly cooked, then move close to the heat for final browning. To fry frozen steak, put it in a greased, pre-heated pan over a low heat. When nearly cooked, increase the heat and brown the meat on both sides.

### Stews

These can be cooked in quantity and then frozen in suitable portions to suit your family requirements. Remember to cook the stew for a little less than the usual time; the re-heating will finalise the cooking. Make sure there is plenty of sauce or gravy to cover the meat or it may dry out. Root vegetables other than onions are best added towards the end of the cooking time as they tend to go mushy. Don't season too heavily; this can be adjusted when re-heating. Flour used for thickening may cause curdling during the re-heating. You can either substitute cornflour or thicken the sauce when re-heating by adding kneaded butter. This is a liaison of butter and flour worked together to a smooth paste - use 1 oz (30 g) butter to ½ oz (15 g) flour - then added, a little piece at a time, to the hot stew and blended in.

Before being frozen, the stew should be cooled and any surplus fat removed. It can then be frozen in foil dishes, plastic boxes or foil-lined casserole dishes. To do this, line the dish in which you intend to re-heat the casserole with foil, leaving enough to fold over the top. Tip the stew into it, lightly cover with overhanging foil and freeze. Turn out of the dish, wrap foil tightly round the frozen block and return it to the freezer. To re-heat, thaw slightly until foil can be removed and return the meat shape to its original dish.

To freeze a bulk quantity of stew (four or six times your family's meal size) turn it into a large roasting tin. Open-freeze in tin until almost solid, then mark into four or six with knife. When completely solid cut into brick-shaped pieces with freezer knife. Wrap each brick in foil, label and stack in freezer.

RECOMMENDED FREEZER LIFE: 6 weeks if bacon, ham or pork are used; 4 months for other meats.

TO USE: re-heat slowly from frozen.

## Stock

Make stock in the usual way, strain, leave until cold and remove the fat. To save freezer space it's a good idea to reduce the stock right down by boiling – you can reduce the stock by two-thirds. Freeze the concentrated stock in ice cube trays, then pack the cubes into polythene bags and return to the freezer.

RECOMMENDED FREEZER LIFE: 6 months.

TO USE: heat gently from frozen and dilute to taste.

## Strawberries

These are not entirely satisfactory frozen whole as they become mushy on thawing. They do, however, make a lovely purée for use as a sauce or to make ice creams or soufflés. To make the purée, simply sieve the clean, dry fruit and stir in sugar to taste. When it has dissolved pack the purée into rigid containers leaving ½-1 in (1-2 cm) headspace, seal and freeze.

If freezing strawberries as whole fruit they are best frozen dry without sugar. Choose firm, dry strawberries – small ones for preference. Hull them, brush off any earth, but don't wash them. Open-freeze strawberries for best results. Spread the fruit out on trays, put in the freezer uncovered and when hard, pack the fruit into polythene bags or rigid containers, seal and return to the freezer.

RECOMMENDED FREEZER LIFE: 1 year.

TO USE: fruit: thaw in containers at room temperature for about 3 hours; serve while still slightly frosty. Purée: thaw at room temperature for about 3 hours and use as required. You can speed up thawing by standing the container in a pan of water. If using the purée hot it may be heated gently from frozen.

## Stuffings

Any recipe for stuffing may be frozen. Divide into required amounts and pack in polythene bags, seal and freeze. If stuffing is to be baked separately, pack in foil dishes, seal and freeze.

Dry forcemeat stuffing mix (breadcrumbs, herbs and seasoning) can be packed in polythene bags and frozen. When needed the required amount can be taken out and mixed with suet and eggs.

RECOMMENDED FREEZER LIFE: completed stuffing, 1 month; dry mix, 6 months; stuffings containing sausage meat, 2 months.

TO USE: completed stuffings: thaw in fridge overnight then stuff meat or fish and cook (if in foil dish, bake from frozen). Dry stuffing: measure out required amount and use direct from freezer.

## Suet

If you have a large amount of fresh suet from a meat carcass, use some of it for making suet puddings. Weigh the rest out into small portions, pack in polythene bags and freeze.

RECOMMENDED FREEZER LIFE: 5 months.

TO USE: thaw and use as fresh.

## Suet Puddings

Savoury or sweet suet puddings can be prepared and cooked - use foil basins if possible - and frozen. When they have cooled, leave them in the basins but replace the tops with fresh foil, overwrap in polythene bags, seal and freeze.

RECOMMENDED FREEZER LIFE: 3 months.

TO USE: boil or steam from frozen until hot - about 2 hours.

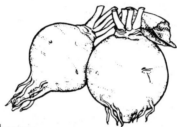

## Swedes/Rutabagas

Trim, peel and cut into dice and blanch for 2 minutes. Cool, drain and pack into polythene bags, seal, label and freeze or mix with other blanched, diced vegetables such as carrots and turnips to make a mixed pack suitable for stews. They can also be frozen puréed. Peel, cut up roughly and cook in boiling, salted water until tender. Sieve and when cool, pack in rigid containers, leaving ½in (1cm) head space. Seal, label and freeze.

RECOMMENDED FREEZER LIFE: 1 year.

TO USE: cook diced rutabaga from frozen in boiling water or add to stews to cook with the meat. Turn purée into a thick pan and re-heat, stirring from time to time.

## Sweetbreads

Wash them thoroughly, then leave to soak in cold water for several hours. Pull off as much of the filament which encloses them as possible, remove the tubes, trim and rinse again, pat dry. Wrap each piece in polythene or freezer paper then pack into polythene bags or rigid containers.

RECOMMENDED FREEZER LIFE: 3 months.

TO USE: thaw in the fridge and use as required.

## Sweetcorn

This is very good to freeze, but do choose fresh, young cobs with pale-coloured, plump, tender kernels. Strip off the leaves and silk threads and trim the stems. Blanch them: 4 minutes for small, 6 minutes for medium and 8 minutes for large. Cool and dry on absorbent paper. Either freeze the whole cobs in polythene bags or scrape off the kernels with a knife and freeze them. Spread the kernels on a tray, place in the freezer and when hard, pack them into a polythene bag, seal and return to the freezer.

RECOMMENDED FREEZER LIFE: 1 year.

TO USE: whole cobs: if cooking from frozen put cobs in cold water, bring to the boil and cook until tender, about 15 minutes. Or allow to thaw for about an hour, then cook in boiling water until tender. Kernels: cook from frozen in boiling water for 5 minutes.

## Tangerines

This is a seasonal fruit but it can be frozen for out-of-season use in fruit salads. Peel and remove pith, divide the fruit into segments, pack in rigid containers and cover with cold sugar syrup. Dissolve 8oz (250g) sugar in 1pt (600ml) water, bring to the boil, remove from heat and allow to cool. Leave ½-1in (1-2cm) headspace, seal and freeze.

RECOMMENDED FREEZER LIFE: 1 year.

TO USE: thaw in container about 3 hours at room temperature and use on its own or add to fruit salads.

**Tarragon**

This herb, particularly good in chicken, fish and egg dishes, freezes well. If you use it often it's worth freezing some. It doesn't need blanching, just wash it, then chop the leaves and freeze in the little plastic containers used for individual portions of jam, or pack into ice cube trays, cover with water and freeze. Tip the frozen cubes into a polythene bag, seal and store in the freezer.

RECOMMENDED FREEZER LIFE: 6 months.

TO USE: add to stews straight from the freezer or thaw and use as required.

**Tea**

You can freeze surplus freshly made strong tea for use in iced tea, fruit cups or punches. Pour the strained tea into ice cube trays and freeze. Pack the frozen cubes into a polythene bag, seal and return to the freezer.

RECOMMENDED FREEZER LIFE: 6 months.

**Tea Cakes**

These are useful to have in the freezer for weekend entertaining or school holidays. Pack in polythene bags and seal well to exclude all excess air, freeze.

RECOMMENDED FREEZER LIFE: 3 months.

TO USE: thaw at room temperature for about 45 minutes or partially thaw, split and toast.

## Thyme

This herb freezes well. Wash and dry – no need to blanch - chop the leaves finely and freeze in the little plastic containers used for individual portions of jam, or pack in foil and freeze. Whole sprigs of thyme are combined with parsley and bay leaves to make bouquets garnis, q.v.

RECOMMENDED FREEZER LIFE: 6 months.

TO USE: add to tomato dishes, pasta and savoury stuffings. Use sparingly.

## Tomatoes

Because of their high water content, tomatoes cannot be frozen for later use in salads - they'll just collapse into pulp when thawed. They are, however, excellent for cooking purposes, so if you grow your own or can buy them cheaply when they're plentiful, freeze them whole, halved, puréed or made into juice.

*Whole:* place them in boiling water for a few seconds, drain them and drop into cold water. The skin will then peel off quite easily. Pack in polythene bags or rigid containers, seal and freeze. If you're in a hurry, simply remove the stems, wipe over the tomatoes, pack and seal. When you come to use them, place the frozen tomatoes into boiling water and in a few seconds the skins will ease off.

*Halved:* if liked they can be cut in halves, spread on a tray and placed in the freezer until hard, then packed in polythene bags or rigid containers and returned to the freezer.

117

*Purée:* use overripe or damaged tomatoes for this. Cut them up roughly, removing any bad parts; no need to skin them. Stew gently with a little salt, pepper and sugar, herbs if liked, such as a bay leaf and marjoram, for 10-15 minutes. Sieve and either pack as it is, or simmer purée until the mixture is thick and the flavour concentrated. Adjust seasoning, cool and pack in rigid containers leaving ½-1 in (1-2 cm) headspace, seal and freeze.

*Tomato juice:* chop up tomatoes, liquidise them, then strain and season with salt. Pack in rigid containers, leaving ½-1 in (1-2 cm) headspace, seal and freeze.

RECOMMENDED FREEZER LIFE: 1 year.

TO USE: whole: add frozen tomatoes to stews, etc. Halves: grill or fry from frozen. Purée: thaw overnight in the fridge or for 3 hours at room temperature and use for soups, stews and sauces. Juice: thaw overnight in the fridge, thin if necessary and adjust seasoning.

See also *Sauces.*

## Tongue

Calves', lambs' and ox tongues can all be frozen raw or cooked. Trim off excess fat and gristle, wash and dry, pack in polythene bags, seal and freeze. If packing a number of small tongues together, wrap each one in moisture-proof paper, then pack a number together in polythene bags.

Ox tongue may be cooked, shaped, weighted and when cold wrapped in foil or polythene, sealed and frozen.

Tongues may also be cooked in a sauce and frozen in this form.

RECOMMENDED FREEZER LIFE: uncooked, 3 months; cooked, 1 month.

TO USE: uncooked: thaw overnight in the fridge and use according to recipe. Cooked: thaw whole tongue in the fridge allowing about 6 hours per lb (500g). Tongues in sauce: gently re-heat from frozen.

## Tripe

This can be frozen uncooked. Wash well in cold water, dry and pack in polythene bags in quantities to suit your family requirements. Seal and freeze. If preferred, cook following a favourite recipe, cool, pack into rigid containers, leaving ½-1 in (1-2 cm) headspace, seal and freeze.

RECOMMENDED FREEZER LIFE: uncooked, 3 months; cooked, 1 month.

TO USE: thaw overnight in fridge and cook or re-heat.

## Trout

Like all fish, this must be absolutely fresh for freezing. Gut the fish, remove the head, tail and fins if necessary. Wash well under running cold water and drain. Wrap each fish closely in a polythene bag, exluding as much air as possible, seal and freeze.

RECOMMENDED FREEZER LIFE: 2 months.

TO USE: cook from frozen.

## Turbot

This can be frozen provided it is absolutely fresh. Remove head, tail and fins. Scrape the belly cavity. Wash thoroughly under running cold water and drain. The fish can be left whole, divided into fillets or cut into steaks. Wrap each piece closely in a polythene bag, seal and freeze.

RECOMMENDED FREEZER LIFE: 2 months.

TO USE: a whole fish should be thawed in the fridge, allowing about 5 hours per lb (500 g); fillets and steaks can be cooked from frozen.

## Turkey

These take up a lot of freezer space so it's not a good idea to store them for too long. It's useful, however, to be able to buy one before the Christmas rush when it will probably be cheaper and store it in the freezer. You'll often find them fairly cheap after Christmas, too, so you could buy and store one for Easter. A ready-frozen turkey should be put in the freezer as soon as possible after buying.

Left-over roast turkey can be sliced and frozen. Interleave the slices with moisture-proof paper and pack them tightly together in a rigid container or polythene bag to prevent them drying out. Or the meat can be chopped, mixed with a sauce and frozen in rigid containers for later use in pancakes, pies or with rice or pasta.

Use the carcass to make stock or soup, which can also be packed in rigid containers and frozen. Don't forget to leave ½-1 in (1-2 cm) headspace for expansion.

RECOMMENDED FREEZER LIFE: uncooked bird, 6 months; cooked meat, 1 month.

TO USE: uncooked bird: thaw it completely in the fridge before cooking. Small birds will take about 2 days, larger ones, 3-4 days. Cooked meat to be eaten cold should be thawed in the container in the fridge; meat in sauce can be gently re-heated from frozen.

**Turnips**

Choose young, tender turnips, trim and peel them. If small, they can be left whole and blanched for 4 minutes. Large ones should be cut into small dice and blanched for 2 minutes. Cool, drain and pack in polythene bags, seal and freeze. They can also be frozen puréed. Trim and peel, cut into slices or dice, cook until tender, drain and mash. Cool, pack into rigid containers, leaving ½-1 in (1-2 cm) headspace, seal and freeze.

RECOMMENDED FREEZER LIFE: 1 year.

TO USE: cook from frozen in boiling water; cooked: gently re-heat purée in a thick pan.

# V

## Vanilla

When flavouring cakes, ice creams, puddings or fillings
with vanilla use only the pure extract, vanilla sugar or a
vanilla pod. Synthetic vanilla flavouring deteriorates in
the freezer.

## Veal

The lean, firm flesh of veal freezes well but it is so expensive
that few people would want to buy a whole carcass. So
choose just the cuts you use and enjoy and buy or order
these from your own butcher or a freezer centre. Shoulder and
breast are useful for roasting or a blanquette; pie veal for
goulash, stews, meat balls, pâtés and, of course, pies; fillet
to cut into escalopes for a quick, easy and delicious,
though expensive meal.

RECOMMENDED FREEZER LIFE: 6 months.

TO USE: thaw overnight in the fridge and use as recipe
directs.

## Vegetables

The glut crop of vegetables you sometimes get in the
garden or are able to take advantage of and buy cheaply
from a local farmer are excellent to freeze. Most vegetables
can be frozen in their raw state very satisfactorily.
Exceptions are tomatoes, lettuce and salad vegetables like
cucumber, white cabbage, watercress, and potatoes, which
must be cooked before freezing. It's not necessary to blanch
vegetables if you're going to use them fairly quickly and
don't object to a slight loss of texture. But for longer storage
and peak condition on thawing it's vital to blanch first.
Listed here are the vegetables you're most likely to grow

121

and freeze with blanching times for 1lb (500g) weight in each case:

Artichokes (Globe): 7 minutes; Lima Beans: 2 minutes; String Beans: 1-2 minutes; Runner Beans: 2 minutes; Broccoli: 3 minutes; Brussels Sprouts: 3-4 minutes; Cabbage: 1½ minutes; Carrots: (whole) 3 minutes, (diced) 2 minutes; Cauliflower: 2 minutes; Kale: 3 minutes; Kohlrabi: 3 minutes; Leeks: 2-4 minutes; Marrow: 3 minutes; Okra: 3-4 minutes; Onions: (chopped) 2 minutes, (small whole) 3 minutes; Parsnips: 2 minutes; Peas: 1 minute; Peppers: (slices) 2 minutes, (halves) 3 minutes; Red Cabbage 1½ minutes; Shallots: 2 minutes; Sweetcorn: (small) 4 minutes, (medium) 6 minutes, (large) 8 minutes; Swiss Chard: 2 minutes; Turnips: (small, whole) 4 minutes, (diced) 2 minutes; Zucchini: 1 minute.

Beetroot, pumpkin and spinach will freeze; they should not be blanched, but cooked lightly and packed in rigid containers. Mushrooms should be tossed in butter. Sweetcorn is the only vegetable which is best cooked in cold water.

### Vegetables, Mixed
Stew packs of mixed vegetables are useful to have in the freezer. Blanch the required vegetables - carrots, turnips, onions - diced or cut small, then mix and pack in polythene bags in the amounts you are likely to need, seal and freeze.

RECOMMENDED FREEZER LIFE: 1 year.

TO USE: add to stews and casseroles from frozen.

### Venison
It's perhaps unlikely that you'll be on the receiving end of a carcass of venison but should one come your way this is the way to deal with it. Clean the shot wounds carefully, then hang it in a cool place for 7-14 days, wiped over with milk every other day to keep the meat fresh. Cut it into joints, getting your butcher to do this if possible. Pack the joints - bones padded with foil where necessary - into polythene bags, seal and freeze. Joints of venison are

sometimes available at freezer centres, or your butcher may be able to get some for you.

RECOMMENDED FREEZER LIFE: 8 months.

TO USE: thaw in the fridge, allowing 5 hours per lb (500g). It's a good idea to pour a marinade over the meat while it is thawing as venison is inclined to be rather dry.

*Venison marinade:* Combine in a pan ¼ pint (150 ml) red wine, 2 tbs olive oil, a sliced onion, a bouquet garni, 8 crushed peppercorns and 1 tbs wine vinegar. Bring to the boil, remove from the heat and leave until cold. Pour over the venison and leave overnight. If liked, the marinade can be strained, reduced to half quantity by rapid boiling and added to the gravy or sauce.

## Vol-au-vent Cases (Patty Shells)

These puff pastry cases are excellent for the freezer – preferably unbaked as they are not so fragile that way. As well as being served hot or cold with a savoury filling, they can be used to make a cold dessert with fruit and whipped cream.

Roll the pastry out to ½in (1cm) thickness, and using a 7in (18cm) plate or saucepan lid as a guide, cut round it with a sharp knife held at a slightly oblique angle. Turn the pastry over and mark out a 6in (15cm) circle with a knife cutting through half the depth of the pastry.

Open-freeze the unbaked cases and when hard, interleave them with squares of moisture-proof paper and pack into polythene bags or rigid containers, seal and return to the freezer. Baked cases should be packed in rigid containers and labelled 'Fragile'.

RECOMMENDED FREEZER LIFE: unbaked, 3 months; baked, 6 months.

TO USE: bake raw cases direct from the freezer in a hot oven then fill them. Leave baked cases at room temperature for about an hour and re-heat if liked for 5-10 minutes before filling.

## Waffles

If you use these regularly you could make a large batch and freeze them to use over several weeks. Bake as usual - don't overbrown them - and when they are cold, pack in required quantities in polythene bags, or stack them in rigid containers, seal and freeze.

RECOMMENDED FREEZER LIFE: 2 months.

TO USE: re-heat from frozen under the grill or in the oven at 375°F (190°C) for about 10 minutes until well browned.

## Walnuts

Shelled, these will keep fresh and moist for a year in the freezer. They can be frozen in halves or chopped but should not be salted. Pack in foil or small cartons and freeze.

RECOMMENDED FREEZER LIFE: 1 year.

TO USE: thaw at room temperature for 3 hours.

## Water Chestnuts

If you have some water chestnuts left over after opening a can, you can pack them into a small plastic container with their own liquor, cover and freeze them.

RECOMMENDED FREEZER LIFE: 3 months.

TO USE: thaw at room temperature.

## Watercress

This won't freeze to use raw as a salad ingredient but it can be made into a savoury butter or soup and frozen.

FOODS

*Watercress butter:* 4 oz (100 g) butter, 2 tbs chopped watercress, a squeeze of lemon juice. Work the butter and the watercress together until well blended, season with salt and pepper and a squeeze of lemon juice. Shape into a roll and wrap in freezer paper. Pack into a plastic bag or overwrap in foil and freeze.

RECOMMENDED FREEZER LIFE: 3 months.

TO USE: cut off the number of slices you need, re-wrap the still hard roll and return it to the freezer.

*Watercress soup:* melt an ounce (30 g) of butter in a saucepan, add an onion and 2 potatoes, peeled and chopped, and sauté them gently for about 5 minutes, cover with a pint (600 ml) of chicken stock. Wash, dry and chop 2 bunches of watercress and add to the pan. Cover with lid and simmer for about 15 minutes. Sieve or blend the soup and adjust the seasoning. Allow to cool then pack in rigid containers, leaving ½-1 in (1-2 cm) headspace, seal and freeze.

RECOMMENDED FREEZER LIFE: 3 months.

TO USE: tip the frozen soup into a saucepan, add a pint (600 ml) of milk and heat through gently. Check seasoning before serving.

**Water Ices or Sherbet**

These can be stored in the freezer for a short time but they don't take long to make if you've a supply of soft fruits in the freezer, or better still fruit purée. To make a blackberry, blackcurrant, raspberry or strawberry water ice take ½ pt (250 ml) purée out of the freezer and leave it to thaw at room temperature for about 4 hours. While it's thawing make a syrup by dissolving 3 oz (75 g) sugar in ½ pt (250 ml) water, bring to the boil and boil for 5 minutes, then leave to cool. Stir the cold syrup into the thawed purée, pour into rigid containers or an ice cube tray and freeze until mushy. Take it out of the freezer and beat well. Freeze in a rigid container.

RECOMMENDED FREEZER LIFE: 2 months.

TO USE: remove from the freezer about 15 minutes before serving.

FOODS

## Whitebait and Smelts

These are the young or fry of the herring or sprat. They're about an inch (2cm) long and are eaten whole - heads, tails, bones. Absolutely fresh ones can be frozen. Put them in a colander and rinse well under running cold water. Drain them and pat dry. Open-freeze them on a tray until hard, then tip them into a polythene bag, seal and return to the freezer.

RECOMMENDED FREEZER LIFE: 2 months.

TO USE: thaw, dry, toss in flour and deep fry a few at a time in hot fat.

## White Currants

These are closely related to redcurrants but are sweeter with a distinct flavour. Strip the fruit off the stalks, wash if necessary and dry. Spread out on trays and open-freeze. When hard, pack into polythene bags, seal and return to the freezer. If preferred, they can be frozen with sugar - 4oz (125g) to 1lb (500g) fruit. Mix the two together then pack into polythene bags and freeze.

RECOMMENDED FREEZER LIFE: 1 year.

TO USE: thaw about 3 hours at room temperature or cook from frozen. Good in fruit salads.

**White Sauce.** See *Sauces.*

## Whiting

A white fish with a delicate flavour, it must be absolutely fresh for freezing. Scale the fish by scraping with a knife from tail to head. Rinse thoroughly then remove the gut, gills and fins. Head and tail can be left on. Wash well under running cold water and drain. Wrap each fish closely in a polythene bag to exclude as much air as possible and freeze.

RECOMMENDED FREEZER LIFE: 3 months.

TO USE: cook from frozen or thaw in the fridge and use according to recipe being followed.

## Wild Duck

Hang wild duck before freezing for the same length of time as you would for immediate use. This is about 3 days. Then pluck and draw it. Wipe with a damp cloth, truss it and pack into a polythene bag, extracting as much air as possible and freeze.

RECOMMENDED FREEZER LIFE: 6 months.

TO USE: thaw overnight in the fridge in its wrappings allowing 5 hours per lb (500 g).

## Wine

If you have some opened wine left over after a party pour it into small cartons, seal and freeze. It can be used at a later date to enrich a casserole.

RECOMMENDED FREEZER LIFE: 2 months.

TO USE: add to casserole while still frozen.

## Woodcock

This small game bird should be plucked but not drawn before freezing. Pack into a polythene bag, extracting as much air as possible, seal and freeze.

RECOMMENDED FREEZER LIFE: 6 months.

TO USE: thaw overnight in the fridge in its wrappings, allowing 5 hours per lb (500 g).

## Yeast

It's not always possible to buy fresh yeast, so if you do a lot of yeast baking it's worth buying a quantity and storing it in the freezer.

Divide into ½oz or 1 oz (15 or 30 g) cubes and wrap each cube in foil, then put them all together in a polythene bag, seal and freeze.

RECOMMENDED FREEZER LIFE: 1 month.

TO USE: thaw cube at room temperature for 30 minutes, or put it straight into lukewarm water and activate as usual.

## Yoghurt

Fruit-flavoured yoghurts store reasonably well in the freezer, but they do tend to separate on thawing, though whipping will improve the texture. Yoghurt with honey freezes very well.

As, however, yoghurt is now so widely available and keeps well in a fridge there seems little point in freezing it.

If you live a long way from the shops the frozen yoghurt which has been prepared commercially would be a good buy.

RECOMMENDED FREEZER LIFE: 1 month.

TO USE: thaw overnight in the fridge.

## Yorkshire Pudding

A supply of these in the freezer would mean one less job to do on a Sunday morning, or they could be used to bolster up a sausage or main meal during the week.

Make up a Yorkshire pudding batter in the usual way and bake it in small patty tins. When they are crisp and golden remove to a cake rack and leave to cool. Open-freeze on a tray and when hard, pack into polythene bags, seal and return to the freezer.

RECOMMENDED FREEZER LIFE: 2 months.

TO USE: replace frozen puddings in patty tin or place on a greased baking sheet and re-heat (375°F, 190°C) for about 10 minutes.

## Youngberries

These are a cross between loganberries and blackberries, grown and trained as the latter. When ripe, the fruit is purplish black. Wash it if necessary and pat dry before packing into polythene bags. Add sugar if liked, about 4oz (125g) per lb (500g) fruit, seal and freeze. Or you can open-freeze the fruit on trays and when it is hard, pack into polythene bags, seal and return to the freezer.

RECOMMENDED FREEZER LIFE: 1 year.

TO USE: thaw overnight in the fridge or 3 hours at room temperature or cook slowly from frozen.

## Zucchini

Use young zucchini about 3 in (7.5cm) long. Wipe with damp cloth, trim ends and cut into ½-in (1-cm) slices. Blanch for 1 minute, cool, drain and open-freeze, or sauté in butter for 1 minute. Cool in fridge, pack into rigid containers leaving ½-1 in (1-2cm) headspace or into polythene bags.

RECOMMENDED FREEZER LIFE: 1 year.

TO USE: blanched: cook from frozen in boiling water or thaw in a colander so they remain firm. Use as your recipe directs.

Sautéed in butter: finish cooking in butter until tender and golden brown.

# DICTIONARY
## OF
## FREEZER
## TERMS

## Air

If food stored in the freezer is in contact with air for any length of time the taste and texture will eventually be affected. Even a small amount trapped accidentally inside the package will cause dehydration, and possibly rancidity. So strong packaging, with no air inside, and secure sealing, so that no air from the freezer can get in, are essential.

See *Freezing Fresh Food, Packaging, Sealing.*

## Alarm

Most freezers have a warning light to tell you if the temperature has risen past $0°$ F ($-18°$ C). But if the freezer is out of sight in a garage or shed you can attach it by a long lead to a warning buzzer that will sound indoors if there's trouble. There are several inexpensive devices that you can buy. They are battery-operated, so remember to check the battery from time to time.

## Aluminium Foil

Foil is moisture- and vapour-proof, but it can be torn and damaged easily. It is particularly useful for wrapping awkwardly shaped food such as joints of meat. The thinner kitchen foil should be used double, so that it will not be torn, or covered with an overwrap. Thicker freezer foil is stronger and can be bought in rolls, or in shaped containers that can go straight from freezer to oven. There are pudding and pie dishes, loaf tins, flan dishes and divided trays for individual meals. Acidic foods can cause pitting in foil, so it is best to use the foil dishes in vinyl coating for fruits. Some can be bought with their own lids, others need to be overwrapped with foil or polythene. Wash the dishes and use them again, being careful to keep their shape. For liquids you can buy foil bags.

Use foil also to line casserole dishes before cooking for the freezer, so that you can remove the dish after the food is frozen and keep the dish in circulation.

See *Packaging.*

133

## Ambient Temperature

Term used to describe the warmth of the air around the freezer. The ambient temperature will be too high if your freezer is next to a heat source or in direct sunlight, and so the freezer will have to work extra hard, thereby using more electricity, to keep its internal temperature at the correct 0°F (−18°C). Extreme cold will affect the working of the freezer's motor, and humidity should also be avoided as it will cause rust.

See *Siting*.

## Ascorbic Acid

Used to retain the colour in light-coloured fruits that may go brown easily. The synthetic form of vitamin C, you can buy it in tablets or crystals which are easier to dissolve. Add ¼tsp per pt (500ml) of cold sugar syrup and pour it over the fruit. Fruit for diabetics or slimmers can be dipped for 15 minutes in a solution of ¼tsp (500mg) in ¼pt (150ml) per lb (500g) of fruit, and packed dry, or packed in a solution of ¼tsp (500mg) per pt (500ml) of water.

## Automatic Defrost

Some fan-assisted upright freezers have systems for automatic defrosting, like a fridge. They save this particular chore, but are much more expensive to buy than other models, and also cost more to run.

## Baskets

Usually sold with a chest freezer, but they can be bought separately. Those that slide across the freezer can save some lifting. Group foods of one type together in each basket to save time spent in searching. Cardboard boxes with handles, or large plastic shopping bags, can perform the same job.

## Blanching

Vegetables need to be scalded for an exact length of time to

134

destroy enzymes (the chemicals that can affect their colour, flavour and texture and destroy vitamin C). Too little blanching means the enzymes won't be killed, too much will spoil the flavour, colour and crispness of the vegetables. After being blanched the vegetables must immediately be chilled, so they don't have a chance to go on cooking in the centre. Vitamin C leaks away into water, so as soon as the vegetables are chilled, they should be drained.

*Steam blanching:* this method takes longer and should not be used for leafy green vegetables, but you may prefer it for delicate items such as cauliflower and asparagus. It will also conserve more vitamins and minerals. Steam the vegetables for half as long again as for water blanching.

*Fruit:* light fruits that discolour easily can be blanched or cooked before freezing. If you don't want to cook, blanch sliced apples ½-1 minute; peaches ½-1 minute; rhubarb 1 minute; poach pears in syrup 2 minutes; blackcurrants can be blanched for ½ minute to soften the skins.

See *Blanching Vegetables.* See also *Unblanched Vegetables.*

## Blast Freezing

This freezing process, which can only be done commercially, reduces the food to very cold temperatures in a very short time and preserves the quality well.

**Boil-in Bags.** See *Polythene.*

## Breakdown

If the machine is 'dead', check that the plug has not been pulled out of its socket or loosened, that the thermostat has not been altered (possibly by a child), that the fuse in the plug, or the one in the fuse box has not blown, or that there is not a power failure locally, or in the house. Only after making these checks, call a service man.

See *Servicing.*

## Brick Freezing

By freezing food in brick shapes whenever possible, you

135

utilise freezer space to the best advantage. Turn a quantity of mince into a large square foil dish or roasting tin. Open-freeze until almost firm, then mark and cut into bricks. Wrap each brick in foil and stack in the freezer.

You can also make bricks of purées, soups and sauces. Use a gusseted polythene bag to line a sugar carton, pour in the liquid and freeze before removing the carton, sealing and stacking in the freezer.

### Bulk-buying

You can economise both in money and in time by making bulk purchases, but it is no good spending money on foods simply because they are cheap. It may be that the quality is poor and the supplier is simply trying to get rid of that item: the freezer will not improve poor quality foods. Or the food may be something that your family does not like, or will not manage to eat up within the recommended storage time. With this in mind, shop carefully for good food.

You can find good value at freezer centres, and in the frozen food departments of supermarkets in meat, poultry and convenience foods. Frozen food delivery services are useful in country districts – look for them in the Yellow Pages. You can order from their list, which will cover every type of food, and although there will be a minimum cost, this is often surprisingly low.

The Yellow Pages will also give you the names of meat suppliers. You will be able to buy fresh, or preferably blast-frozen, at good prices, and the meat may be delivered too. If the supplier has a shop, you will be able to check before-hand that his quality is good. If you are bulk-buying meat from your butcher, check whether he will freeze down the meat for you or allow you to collect it in batches over several days. Remember a freezing-down capacity is normally one-tenth of the total capacity in any 24-hour period. Freeze down the more perishable cuts such as mince and offal first then chops, steaks and finally the joints. Choose the cuts of meat you know your family prefers, and try to have joints boned and rolled as they take up less freezer space. Meat used to be cheaper at certain times of the year, but this does not happen so much now. However, it is always worth looking around for a sudden drop in prices, or asking your butcher to keep you informed of bargain offers.

Fish has to be frozen within 24 hours of being caught, so you are not likely to bulk-buy it for freezing unless you live on the coast.

Vegetables and fruit that have been in a shop will not be freshly harvested, so are not worth freezing unless they are seasonally cheap imported foods. 'Pick-your-own' farms offer good value and you may be able to buy direct from market gardens or farms. On market day, too, you can bid for fresh-picked bulk buys of fruit and vegetables.

Remember that you do not have to be overwhelmed by buying in bulk – it often pays to share food (and transport) with friends.

A useful time-saver to bulk buy is bread. Buy the family's needs for a week or two and pop it into the freezer to save unnecessary shopping trips.

## Capacity

The size of a freezer is indicated by its gross volume, measured in cubic feet, or, more normally now, litres. 1 cu ft is equal to 28.3 l. The *storage capacity*, that is the amount of food that can be stored, will be less than that figure, and will vary according to the type of food and how it is packed – an awkwardly shaped joint and round containers will take up more space than a neat stack of square containers. Manufacturers calculate storage capacity by allowing for an average packing density of 20lb (10kg) or sixteen 1pt (500ml) cartons per cu ft (28.3 l).

*Freezing capacity* refers to the amount of fresh food that can be frozen in a 24-hour period and is usually a tenth of the total storage capacity. Some machines can cope with more than this, as will be seen from the manufacturers' instructions.

## Carbon Dioxide

In the form of dry ice, this will keep food frozen while it is being transported, or during a prolonged power cut, but in normal circumstances you would not be likely ever to need it. It should not be allowed to come into contact with the food or its packaging, and you should always wear heavy gloves to handle it.

## Cellophane or Plastic Wrap

The ordinary kitchen type is too thin to be used in the freezer on its own, but is very useful for wrapping items separately which are then packed all together in a polythene bag. Freezer film is double thickness and is suitable to use. It is more expensive than polythene, but is a very quick and efficient way of wrapping sandwiches or rolls, and for overwrapping lidless containers.

## Chest Freezers

Less expensive to make than uprights, and therefore less expensive to buy. Cheaper to run too, because they don't lose so much cold air when the freezer is opened. Less maintenance because they will need defrosting only once or twice a year, but chest freezers may be difficult for a small woman or someone with back trouble to manage – it's quite a way to grope down to the bottom, and lifting out baskets to reach what is stored below can be a job for a weightlifter. However, they can be more closely packed than an upright.

A chest freezer in the kitchen can provide a useful working surface if its top is covered with laminate, or if it is mounted on rollers so that it can slide out from under the counter top. Otherwise it may be difficult to find room for a chest type, but suitable places could be a cellar, landing or spare room indoors, or a garage outside.

If the freezer is in the kitchen you will see from the warning light if the temperature is too high, but otherwise you may feel safer if you have a warning device – a battery-operated buzzer that can be connected to the freezer outside or upstairs and will sound in the kitchen if the temperature goes too high. Some chest freezers have a lock and key, so they will be secure in an outhouse.

Chest freezers normally have a separate fast-freeze compartment so that you don't have the chore of moving other packages out of the way before stacking fresh food along the bottom and sides.

When buying, look for extras: drain hole, storage baskets, interior light, laminated work surface, rollers, lock and key.

See *Siting*.

## China

Your sturdier plates, jugs, will not be damaged if you put them into the freezer – you can open-freeze on a meat dish, for instance. Casseroles can be used in the oven after being in the freezer as long as you allow them to come to room temperature first; but this would probably take too long for the safety of the food inside, and anyway you will want your casserole for continued use in the kitchen, so most cooks line the dish with foil before cooking and freezing and return the dish to the cupboard. Pyrosil is a toughened ceramic that will go from freezer straight to the oven – it costs more, but it is useful for cook-ahead entertaining.

## Chinagraph

Type of pencil that will write directly onto polythene and foil and will not fade in the freezer. Writes most easily if it is slightly warmed.

## Colour Code

To save unnecessary rummaging through packs it is helpful to devise a colour code system – red for meat, blue for fish, green for vegetables, orange for fruit, yellow for cooked dishes, for example. Some manufacturers make polythene bags striped in these colours, or you can buy coloured ties, labels or freezer tape.

### Compressor

This is the part of the freezer that changes the pressure of the refrigerant and also pumps it round. It is a kind of motor and should function for at least ten years without giving any problems. A faulty one would show up during the first year and would be covered by the manufacturer's warranty.

See *How a Freezer Works, Insurance, Servicing.*

### Condenser

In this part of the freezer, gas is condensed into a liquid (the refrigerant) and the heat given off into the surrounding air. There are three types of condenser: skin type, where the condenser tubes are under the lining of the cabinet, fan-assisted and static plate (tubes at the back of upright freezers and refrigerators). Fan-assisted and static plate types need to have the build-up of dust brushed off about every six months. Fan-assisted condensers can cope with more food for fast freezing than other types in relation to the size, and can cope with a higher ambient temperature but are a little noisier and may be prone to condensation. Freezers with skin condensers will feel warm to the touch.

### Conservator

These are used mainly by shops to keep products cold, or by, for instance, kennels who bulk-buy large quantities of frozen meat. They are not normally of value in the home because they are not capable of fast-freezing fresh food – so beware of buying a second-hand one, mistaking it for a conventional freezer.

### Cooking From Frozen

Many foods can be cooked from frozen. Some, like chicken, must be thawed first; others, like meat, can either be cooked from frozen or thawed. More about cooking from frozen in the chapter of that name.

### Cross-flavouring

Some highly flavoured or seasoned foods can transfer their

flavour to others. Culprits are garlic, cheese and onion-flavoured dishes, curries and raw onion. Secured double or extra-thick wrappings will prevent this happening.

**Cubic Capacity.** See *Capacity*.

## Defrosting

Frost and ice will build up inside the freezer and should be regularly removed. Between full-scale defrosting sessions keep it down by scraping off as much as you can once a week with a plastic or wooden spatula – never metal. Make particularly sure that there is no ice preventing the lid or door from closing properly. A chest type will need defrosting only once or twice a year; an upright one more often – three or four times a year. This is also a good time to dust the condenser tubes.

See Basic Freezer Management.

## Dehydration

This is the removal of moisture from food and occurs if it hasn't been properly wrapped. Meat particularly can become tough and dry through contact with air, so always wrap closely in moisture- and vapour-proof wrapping.

## Discoloration

The light-coloured fruits, vegetables (such as cauliflower) and fish will discolour easily, especially when they are thawed. Protect them by dipping them in a solution of lemon juice – 1 lemon to 1½pt (1 l) of water – or ascorbic acid or salted water. Add lemon juice or salt to blanching water. Pack fruit in syrup or blanch or cook.

Discoloration in frozen meat or fish is caused by faulty packaging which has allowed air to come in contact with the food. The food will not be unsafe, but may taste slightly rancid.

See *Ascorbic Acid, Freezer Burn, Rancidity, Syrup Pack*.

## Dividers

Plastic-covered, L-shaped frames of mesh (like baskets)

that are used in the base of chest freezers to separate the food. Also refers to small pieces of foil, freezer tissue etc. used to separate foods.

See *Interleaving*.

## Door Seal

Most freezers have a magnetic door seal, and it is very important that this is fitting closely. Insert a piece of paper – it should need quite a tug to pull it out. A build-up of frost around the door would show that it was not closing tightly (this could be caused by the freezer not being level, so check this too). Try your own repair – stick-on draught-excluder foam behind the door seal, sometimes referred to as the gasket. If this is not enough contact the manufacturer for a new seal.

## Drip Loss

This term refers to the liquid that is lost from foods when they are thawed. It happens particularly with meat, which should be cooked immediately it has thawed to prevent too much loss. Drip contains goodness, so it should be used if possible, in gravy. Fast freezing and slow thawing will cut down drip loss.

**Dry Ice.** See *Carbon Dioxide*.

## Dry Pack

Fruits that do not discolour badly – the darker ones such as raspberries, strawberries, currants – can be packed just as they are (without washing, if possible) without sugar or sugar syrup. Leave ½ in (1 cm) headspace. A rigid container protects soft fruits.

See *Ascorbic Acid, Open-freezing*.

## Dry Sugar Pack

Fruits that will not discolour can be packed with sugar coating, so that thawing will produce a delicious fruity syrup. Coat the fruit by rolling it with fruit sugar on a sheet of greaseproof paper, or pack in layers, finishing with

sugar, in a rigid container. Leave ½in (1 cm) headspace.
See *Open-freezing*.

## Electricity, Use Of

As a rough guide, a freezer is estimated to use about 2 units
of electricity per cu ft (28.31) per week. A small model uses
slightly more in proportion to its size than a large one, and
an upright uses more than a chest type because it loses more
cold air when the door is opened. It's possible to reduce the
running costs to about 1.5 units per cu ft (28.31) if you keep
the freezer in a cool, dry place, make sure it is well filled and
don't keep the door open longer than is necessary.

## Enzymes

These are chemicals that are present and necessary in all
living cells. After harvesting, the enzymes in fruit and
vegetables continue to be active, in vegetables causing loss
of colour and changes in flavour, and in fruit causing
discoloration. The temperature in a freezer is not low
enough to stop this activity, but a high temperature will
halt it, and this is why vegetables have to be blanched before
freezing. Dark fruits do not discolour, but lighter ones
must be cooked, blanched or packed in a cold syrup pack.
Vitamin C (ascorbic acid) also helps to stop discoloration.
The enzymes present in other foods do not cause such
problems, except those in fatty foods which contribute to
rancidity.

See *Ascorbic Acid, Blanching, Dry Pack, Rancidity,
Syrup Pack*.

## Fast-freeze

The faster you freeze fresh food, the better its quality is
protected. The process of freezing leads to the formation of
ice crystals inside each cell of the food, and slow freezing
produces large crystals which rupture the cell walls and
result in collapsed, mushy food on thawing. A certain
amount of liquid loss, known as 'drip' is bound to happen,
with meat and fruit particularly, but because fast freezing
makes smaller ice crystals, there will be less drip

afterwards. Most freezers now have a fast-freeze switch which overrides the thermostat so that the motor goes on operating to keep the temperature below the normal setting (0° F, −18° C) to less than −18° F, −28° C. If there is no fast-freeze switch, adjust the thermostat to its coldest setting.
See The Fast-freeze Switch.

### Flavourings

Synthetic flavouring becomes stronger in the freezer, particularly vanilla, so it is best to halve the quantities.
See *Spices*.

### Flowers

Roses are the only flowers we've frozen successfully.
See *Roses*.

**Foil.** See *Aluminium Foil, Packaging*.

**Free-flow.** See *Open-freezing*.

### Freezer Burn

If the surface of meat has greyish-white marks on it, this is a sign that the meat has not been wrapped carefully enough, so that it has become dehydrated through contact with air. There may also be some rancidity through oxidation, but it will not be enough to spoil the meat, which will be perfectly safe to eat. 'Dry' cooking, such as roasting or grilling, may leave the texture of the meat tough and dry, but after stewing no one will notice the difference.

### Freezer Life

This is the time a food can spend in the freezer without its quality, flavour or texture being affected.
See *Storage Times*.

### Freezer Tape

Adhesive tape with special glue that does not come unstuck at low temperatures. Use for tying bags, sealing loose lids and sticking on labels. Can be bought in several colours.

### Freezing Capacity

The amount of food that a freezer can freeze down from fresh in 24 hours. Usually ten per cent of the storage capacity, but check manufacturer's instructions.
See *Capacity*.

### Freezing Coils

The evaporator coil, which is the part of the system that picks up heat from the cabinet to reduce the temperature inside.
See *How a Freezer Works*.

### Freezing Fresh Food

Do not aim to freeze more than one-tenth of the freezer's storage capacity – or the amount the manufacturer recommends. If food is more than 2 lb (1 kg), switch on to fast-freeze 2-3 hours beforehand. Never introduce warm food into the freezer; it will increase the temperature inside, possibly slightly thawing the frozen packs already in the freezer, and certainly spoiling their quality. So cool food quickly and thoroughly first, in a bowl of cold water for casseroled foods. In hot weather, food can be chilled for a short while in the fridge. Flat packs will allow the food to freeze rapidly. Make sure packaging is moisture- and vapour-proof, and that you have left headspace if necessary. Place the food in the fast-freeze compartment or on the bottom and against the side, leaving space between packs for the air to circulate. Don't allow any of the 'fresh' warm packs to come into contact with those already in the freezer in case you thaw them. Switch off the fast-freeze after 24 hours.

Food will not improve in quality when it is in the freezer, so it is no good freezing tough meat or limp vegetables or fruit and expecting a magical change in them when they come out of the freezer. On the other hand, if you fast-freeze, and wrap securely and use within the recommended storage time the food will be as good in quality when it is

taken out of the freezer as when it went in.
See *Fast-freeze, Packaging, Sealing, Labelling, Head-space*.

## Fridge-freezers

This type combines upright freezer and refrigerator in one unit which cannot be separated, usually with the freezer below. Each unit has its own compressor system, so the unit is not cheap, but it is very useful if space is limited. You can freeze fresh food in them. A fridge-freezer can be useful for a household with a chest freezer in the cellar, so that short-stay items can be kept in the kitchen freezer to avoid too many trips. Large models twin refrigerator and freezer side by side. They can be built in and often team up with an oven for a super-luxury effect.
See *Upright Freezers*.

## Frost

Frost or 'cavity ice' inside packs is caused by bad packaging. Either the air has not been carefully removed during packing, or the pack is punctured and air has entered it. The air has picked up moisture from the food, which will have become dried out.

## Glass

Containers of glass – but not milk bottles – can be used in a freezer. Test them first by freezing them overnight empty in a bag. We have found that they can shatter for no apparent reason, even after they have been used safely for this purpose before – a kind of fatigue affects them, so it is always safest to enclose glass containers in a bag in case of accidents. Best, too, to line with foil or polythene. Don't put cold glass down on a hot surface. Leave headspace in containers, and remember that you won't be able to slip food past the shoulders of a glass jar until it is fully thawed.

## Greaseproof Paper

Not suitable as packing for the freezer – packs of butter

should be overwrapped with foil or polythene. Can be used for separating chops, etc.

## Harvesting

Pick in the early morning, while it is still cool, and choose young, fresh vegetables (peas, beans and sweetcorn must be frozen just before they mature) and fruit that is just ripe – it will not ripen in the freezer. Keep the fruit and vegetables cool and tip them gently onto trays. Freeze immediately if you can; don't leave longer than 12 hours and put them in the fridge if they are to be left longer than 2 hours. Vitamin C is lost very quickly after harvesting, so the faster you can get the produce into the freezer the better. Any imperfect pieces can be puréed and then frozen. Add sugar, if liked, to the fruit purée and ascorbic acid if it may discolour. Pour the purée slowly into containers so that no air bubbles are trapped. Leave headspace.

## Headspace

Liquid expands by one-ninth of its volume when frozen, and this also applies to food that contains a lot of liquid – such as strawberries. So to prevent the pack bursting open, room must be allowed for expansion below the top of a container. Allow about ½in (1 cm) in wide containers, ¾in (2 cm) per pt (500 ml) in narrow containers. If more than this is left, fill the gap with crumpled cellophane or greaseproof paper to block out air. Cover purées with a layer of cling film if they are likely to discolour.

## Heat Sealer

This machine allows you to seal your polythene bags before freezing, or make your own bags from a length of polythene sleeve. A cool iron over paper can be used to heat-seal polythene as well – make sure surfaces are free of food and that no air is trapped inside.

## How a Freezer Works

Working on the principle that heat is attracted by a cold

area (this is why warmth escapes when someone opens the door), the freezer system draws heat from the cabinet. This happens when the liquid in the tubes is changed into a gas. A liquid with a low boiling point (the point at which it turns into gas) is used. This is known as a refrigerant, and is circulated round the freezer casing. The system consists of a compressor which pumps the refrigerant round as well as increasing its pressure, a condenser and evaporator tubes. The refrigerant turns into a gas in the evaporator and picks up heat from the cabinet, goes through the compressor and then into the condenser where it gives off its heat into the room.

## Ice Glazing

Whole fish can be glazed in ice to seal in the flavour and protect in storage. Clean and prepare the fish and open-freeze it until solid. Dip the fish in ice-cold fresh water and a thin film of ice will form over the fish. Return it to the freezer. Repeat about three times at half-hourly intervals. Wrap in heavy-gauge polythene and return to the freezer.

## Installation

A freezer needs a 13 or 15 amp plug and socket. When installing the freezer, make sure the cabinet is level otherwise the lid or door will not be properly closed. Allow it to stand for an hour before switching on, to let any displaced oil return to the compressor. During that hour, wipe the inside with a solution of ½ tbs bicarbonate to 1 pt (500 ml) of warm water. Dry well. When you switch on, check that all the indicator lights are working, then leave the freezer for 24 hours to get to the normal running temperature of 0°F (−18°C). Use a freezer thermometer to check that the temperature is correct, then put in frozen food. If you are freezing fresh food, switch on the fast-freeze switch 2-3 hours before adding the food.

Finally, and most important, tape over the plug so that it cannot be pulled out by mistake. Your insurance policy may not cover you for accidental switching off.

See *Fast-freeze, Freezing Fresh Food.*

## Insulated Containers

Special bags and boxes are available in which you can carry
frozen purchases home, or pack them for picnics or
holidays. The insulation works the other way round for
hot foods too. Adding a thermal bag helps keep food hot or
cold. Use insulated bags to hold food packages when
defrosting.

## Insurance

Freezer insurance plans cover two areas: food and
servicing. You will probably be offered insurance cover
when you buy the freezer, and the most important subject is
food.

The contents of a well-filled freezer should be safe, even
after a power cut of 24 hours, if the lid or door has not been
opened. If the freezer has been unplugged or switched off
through your own fault (turning off electricity before going
on holiday is the most common case) then the food may
have become totally thawed and unusable. You are likely to
find your insurance does not cover you for this.

The small print may also tell you that whereas you are
covered, among other possibilities, for freezer breakdown,
and accidental failure of the public electricity supply,
failure of the electricity supply caused by strikes is another
matter, and you may not be covered. Once again, though,
check carefully what your policy says.

Schemes offered by the shop where you buy the freezer
will be linked with one of the large insurance companies,
or you can extend your house policy to cover food in the
freezer. Remember, though, that a new freezer is not likely
to break down, that power cuts rarely last as long as 24
hours and that as long as you don't switch off by mistake
there is no real likelihood of your food being ruined. But if
you don't want to take the risk, and the worst happens, keep
the food in the freezer – your insurance company may want
to see it.

The other kind of scheme covers breakdown. The manufacturer's warranty extends over the first year, and you
should not have to pay for labour, so you do not need
insurance except to cover food. The compressor is the part

most likely to go wrong (and it would be expensive to replace) though it should last for several years without any problems. Some companies will not insure a machine that is more than 10 years old, or will only do so if it is covered by a service contract.

If the machine breaks down, check with your insurers before getting it mended.

### Interleaving

Use polythene, foil or greaseproof paper between pieces of food – slices of cake or pâté, or chops or fish fillets – when packing, so that you can just take the pieces you need. Chops twisted together can be almost impossible to prise apart without having to thaw more than you want.

See *Open-freezing*.

### Keeping Times. See *Storage Times*.

### Knives

Serrated and extremely sharp knives, some Teflon-coated, are available which will saw and slice frozen food. Butchers' saws and meat cleavers – dangerous, so be careful – are useful if you are preparing meat for the freezer as well as cutting it when frozen. Warming the blade will help in cutting frozen food.

### Labelling

It is essential to label packs before they go into the freezer because they soon adopt heavy disguise, and you don't want the freezer door open longer than necessary while you hunt around. How you label is up to you, but most important is the name of the food and the date. The quantity and any extra cooking instructions or reminders can also be added. You can write directly on to polythene with felt-tip pens or chinagraph. If you are following a colour code you can buy coloured stick-on labels and write with white chinagraph pencil or wax crayon. Stick labels onto bag before filling it with food (or inside bag facing outwards to be sure they won't come off; use freezer tape to secure them). Label the top of the pack if you have a chest freezer, the side if it's an upright.

Some twist ties have a wide flag end for writing on, or you can buy plastic flag ties.

## Left-overs

One of the many boons of a freezer is that left-over food does not have to be thrown away. But don't leave it hanging around for even a few hours before you decide to freeze it. Cool as rapidly as possible so that bacteria do not have a chance to multiply, and freeze immediately it is cold. Some foods may later be used as meals, others as flavouring for new dishes.

## Loading

Stacking food is easier, and less wasteful of space, if the food is packed in square containers. Even liquids in polythene can be stacked in this way if you line a cardboard box with a gusseted bag, pour in the liquid and freeze until solid before removing the carton. Label all packs clearly.

See Correct Freezer Loading.

## Micro-organisms

This term covers mould, yeasts and bacteria. Most are harmless, though some may spoil the quality of the food. At freezer temperatures the micro-organisms survive but cannot multiply – they can only multiply at higher temperatures, particularly at $50°F$ ($10°C$) and above. This is why it is important to wash fruit (blanching vegetables cleans them as well) and cool cooked foods rapidly before freezing them so that they do not stay at room temperature for long. Cooked meat in particular can be susceptible to a type of bacteria that produces poisons that are not destroyed by cooking; re-heated meat is also at risk. Raw poultry may carry salmonella, which is why it must always be thoroughly cooked, and why cooked poultry should not be put down on a surface that has had raw poultry on it. Moulds and yeasts may change the quality of the food, but will not make it unsafe to eat.

## Microwave Thawing

Frozen meat can be defrosted as fast as 2 minutes per lb (500 g), an 8 in (20 cm) diameter cake in 3 minutes, in a domestic microwave oven. Defrosting is achieved by rhythmic switching on and off of the electromagnetic waves (so that it defrosts only, without cooking as well). You can do this pulsing manually, but it is obviously easiest to have the type of oven that has an automatic defrosting control. Plates of glass, china, plastic and paper can safely be used in a microwave oven, but not metal or aluminium foil, which will reflect the microwaves away from the food. Special freezer-to-microwave containers can be bought to overcome this problem.

## Moving

It is sensible to run down stocks in the freezer as much as you can before moving, but it is not necessary to empty it altogether unless the removal men cannot handle it with food (check first) or there is an overnight stop. Switch on the fast-freeze 2-3 hours before you leave, and unplug at the last minute. Refrain from opening the lid during transit or until it has been switched on again and the indicator lights tell you that the temperature is steady at 0°F, −18°C. The food should remain frozen for as long as it takes to move house, but you can take out a special insurance policy to cover moving. If it is not possible to keep the food in the freezer, pack into insulated bags or into tea chests with dry ice (see *Carbon Dioxide*). Make sure the freezer is not stood on its side.

## Noise

Some models are noisier than others. Those with fan-assisted condensers make more noise than those with static plate condensers. Quietest are the skin-type condensers. If the motor seems to be running a great deal, there may be dust on the condenser, or it may be time for a defrosting session. A very noisy compressor could mean there is something wrong, or that the machine is getting old.

## Non-freezers

Bananas, hard-boiled eggs, mayonnaise, custards (except canned), soft meringue toppings, crisp salad greens or radishes, single or unpasteurised cream, soured cream, cottage cheese, canned or bottled drinks, milk (except homogenised) do not freeze well.

## Open-freezing

This method of freezing means that you can measure small quantities from a large pack of free-flow food, as you can with commercially frozen peas. The faster freezing also means that large ice crystals do not have a chance to form in moist foods such as strawberries, which leaves them less mushy on thawing. Delicate items such as iced cakes and pastries and duchesse potatoes also benefit from open-freezing.

Spread the food out on baking trays or large plates, or the specially produced plastic freezer trays, allowing air space around each piece. When the food is hard (you can leave it overnight) pack it into bags or boxes, seal and label. The delicate foods should be unwrapped before being thawed, to avoid being damaged by the wrappings. Open-freezing is also suitable for chops, small fish, fish steaks and fillets.

For rather odorous items like onions and cauliflower, slip the tray inside a roomy polythene bag and seal it loosely while open-freezing.

See *Trays*.

## Packaging

The main function of packaging in the freezer is to protect the quality of the food. If air is allowed to come into contact with the food it will become dehydrated in the case of meat and vegetables, or slightly rancid if it's fatty, and lose colour if it is fruit. No air should be allowed inside the bag, so it must be securely sealed, and strong enough to survive being moved against other packages inside the freezer. There is a good selection of packaging made for the freezer but it can be expensive, so keep other suitable containers: ice cream, margarine and yoghurt pots, and strong polythene bags. Clean them all thoroughly, sterilising packages for extra cleanliness. Cheap containers may be brittle, so cover with polythene bags for extra strength. Make sure that the packaging won't allow air to get inside, or moisture to get out.

See *Aluminium Foil, Labelling, Polythene, Rigid Containers, Sealing, Waxed Cartons.*

## Plastic. See *Polythene.*

## Polythene

You can buy polythene in sheets, in bags of all shapes and sizes or as a long sleeve (see *Heat Sealer*). The bags are cheaper to use than rigid containers, especially if bought in bulk, and can be used for liquids as well as solids if you use gusseted bags to line a square carton, pour in the liquid and freeze before removing the carton. Very thin polythene may be porous and therefore not suitable, and you must be sure that the seams will not split. 120-gauge bags are adequate for short-term storage; and the thicker, 200-gauge bags are best for long-term storage and stand up to wear and tear better, but are more expensive. They are made in all sizes, plain or gusseted, and also in narrow shapes for fish or duck. 300-gauge bags are available for highly flavoured foods, like game. There are also coloured bags to fit your colour code.

Boil-in bags are made from high-density polythene and will stand up to boiling water so that you can heat stews, soups and sauces in them without fear of burning the food – they also cut down on washing-up. Leave space at the top, to allow for expansion.

Polythene sheeting is useful for wrapping meat, and for overwrapping foil or highly flavoured foods.

See *Packaging.*

## Power Cuts

Most are not long enough to affect the food in your freezer. Don't open it during the cut, or for two hours afterwards; and if you are worried, cover it with a blanket or newspapers. The food in a well-stocked freezer should remain frozen for several hours – at least 17 hours for a 12 cu ft (340 l) size. If you have advance warning of a long cut, switch on the fast-freeze switch and move ice cream and cream cakes to the bottom or back of the freezer. If it is not full, fill the space with crumpled newspaper in boxes. After a 24-hour cut check whether anything has become thawed.

See *Re-freezing.*

## Pyrosil. See *China.*

## Rancidity

Fatty foods, such as fatty meats, oily fish, butter and pastry, can become rancid. This is caused by the effect of oxygen in the air on the acids in fat cells on the surface of the food. It does not affect the safety of the food, but it will affect taste and smell. This is why fatty foods have a shorter freezer life than non-fatty foods. Salt speeds up rancidity, so salted butter cannot be stored as long as unsalted, and ham and salty bacon also have a short freezer life. Very careful and secure wrapping, and strong packaging such as the thick, vacuum-packed bags for commercially frozen bacon, and ice glazes for fish help to preserve them for longer periods.

## Re-freezing

Whether or not you can re-freeze depends on how much thawing has taken place. The two problems will be loss of texture and bacterial activity. If loss of texture has occurred there will be no point in re-freezing the food in its present form, but fruit and vegetables can be cooked and puréed for sauces, soups and casseroles, as long as they still smell all right.

Bacterial activity is thought to be increased in food that has been frozen, once the food becomes warm. Vegetables are particularly susceptible, and that is why they must be cooked immediately, even if they are frozen again in cooked form. Food that has been unfrozen for some time will have gone off as any other food does and here, as always, your nose will be a good guide. Fish is a food that deteriorates quickly, so sniff it well. Ice cream and food with synthetic cream must be thrown away.

Food that is still cold to the touch, with ice crystals still remaining it it, will be safe, especially if it is still in its wrapping.

Switch your freezer on to fast-freeze when you are re-freezing food, and use up the foods as soon as possible.

See Thawing and Re-freezing.

## Refrigerant

This is the liquid that circulates round the freezer system. It has to have a very low boiling point. The one usually found in domestic freezers, Freon 12, has a boiling point of 21.7°F, —7°C. Refrigerant can occasionally leak, and this should be covered by your insurance policy.

## Rigid Containers

Invaluable in a freezer because they protect delicate foods (especially useful in a chest freezer) and, with their square and oblong shapes, stack compactly to save freezer space. You can also use them to freeze liquids in convenient shapes. (See *Brick Freezing*.) The containers can be used many times as long as they are carefully washed. However they are not cheap to buy, and it is worth saving the containers of commercial foods to add to your stock. Well-fitted lids are essential for a good seal, so hold them down with freezer tape if necessary. You can buy some containers with coloured lids, to follow your colour code.

See *Headspace, Packaging.*

## Roses

Cut buds when they are just opening, and stand them in warm water for some time. Pack in a rigid container and cover with an ice glaze, or wrap individually in foil, and freeze.

## Rotating Stocks

You should aim to turn stock round two or three times a year, although you may want to keep bulk buys and garden produce longer. If you are buying ahead on a planned monthly or three-monthly basis, rotation should follow automatically. Try to keep the freezer at least three-quarters full to save on running costs, but don't save food unnecessarily like a miser. You'll be using up cooked food, and fatty and oily foods quickly, and you should review the stocks frequently to make sure nothing has been overlooked.

## Running Costs

When computing these, take into account the cost of electricity (about 2 units per cu ft (28.3 l) per week), annual depreciation (say 10 per cent, though a freezer will last at least ten years), food insurance, repairs (they should only be minor ones). Packaging is an item that should also be included in the running costs and, if you are a perfectionist, the interest you might have earned on the cost of the freezer if the money had been invested instead. Against this, of course, you set the savings made by buying food in bulk, and being able to buy ahead of price rises and while seasonal food is cheap – or free, if you are storing your own produce. And, of course, you will be using your car to shop less often.

To keep down the costs of electricity, don't run the freezer at a colder temperature than necessary, don't have it more empty than full, and don't open the door more than you have to.

See *Electricity, Unused Space.*

## Salmonella

This is a type of bacteria that can lead to severe food poisoning. It can be present in poultry, which is why it is important to thaw chicken thoroughly before cooking, so that the heat can penetrate during cooking right to the centre and kill any salmonella bacteria there.

See *Micro-organisms.*

## Salt

As it becomes stronger in taste during freezing, it is best to go easy on the salt when preparing cooked meat dishes, and add more when you re-heat them if it is needed. Salt also has the effect of accelerating rancidity in fatty foods stored in the freezer.

## Sealing

The moisture/vapour-proof rule that applies to packaging is just as important when it comes to sealing the pack, otherwise air will be able to creep inside, and moisture will escape. In bags, simply tying a knot is effective, though you might not be able to untie the knot without damaging the bag, and you may not be able to expel the air effectively. Or twist the bag and tie with string or paper- or plastic-covered wire tie tags, or even electrical wire. Double the top of the bag and double-tie for a sure seal. 'Flag' tie tags have wide ends for labelling. A time-saving gadget is the sealer fitted with adhesive freezer tape – like the one butchers use. Some polythene bags are self-seal, with a top that clips shut. You can also seal polythene bags with a heat sealer or warm iron over paper – be sure there is no air trapped inside, and no food on the inner surfaces.

Rigid containers must have a close-fitting lid – if in doubt, double seal with freezer tape.

See *Heat Sealer, Labelling, Packaging.*

## Separating

Freezing causes some foods to separate: French dressing, plain yoghurt, non-homogenised milk. Brisk stirring, whipping or beating can often improve the texture.

## Servicing

A freezer is not a machine that is prone to break down, and you are likely to be able to use yours for several years without any major repairs being necessary. The most expensive item to replace is the compressor, but if this should be faulty it would show up during the first year, while the freezer is still under the manufacturer's warranty. The manufacturer should replace any parts during this time without charging for the part or for labour. After this period you can enter into a service contract, which will guarantee you 24-hour, seven-days-a-week service with probably a stand-by freezer if it's needed, and food insurance (make sure you think the food allowance is high enough). Or you can take out insurance to cover breakdown repair costs, but you would possibly have to find your own service man. Note that the insurance company would want you to contact them first, if possible. A freezer over 10 years old would probably have to be regularly serviced to qualify for breakdown insurance.

Service contracts and breakdown insurance schemes are more expensive than simple food insurance policies, and add considerably to running costs, so you may prefer to assume that your machine will prove reliable and not enter into a service contract or insurance scheme.

See *Breakdown, Insurance, Re-freezing, Warning Light On*.

## Siting

Space, convenience and the ambient temperature (the warmth of the surrounding air) are the three most important things to consider when you are deciding where to put the freezer. A chest freezer takes up more room than an upright (though you need space for the opening of the door) and you may have more room for a chest type outside the kitchen, for instance in the cellar or garage or in a spare room or on the landing. If the freezer is to go upstairs, make sure that the spot can take the weight of a fully loaded freezer which may be as much as ¼ ton (200kg) and avoid one with a noisy motor (fan-assisted types make the most noise) because you don't want the family to be disturbed at night. Check, too, that there is a 13 or 15 amp socket, and that you can get the freezer to the site (around any sharp corners).

Ambient temperature makes a difference to the electricity bill. In a very warm atmosphere, next to the cooker for instance, or in a hot, sunny spot under a window, the freezer will have to work extra hard to stay cold. The kitchen is obviously the most convenient site, but it may be more sensible to choose a cooler place elsewhere.

A garage must not be too hot (in direct sunlight), too cold or very damp. To protect the freezer from any damp, raise it off the floor on wooden plinths. Leave room for air to circulate round it. If necessary, in damp weather use a fan heater to dry the air. It is not a good idea to cover the freezer with a tarpaulin, but silicone furniture polish will help protect it from rust. A freezer with a fan-assisted condenser is more prone to rust, and is not best suited to a garage. An interior light is a useful accessory for a freezer in a dark position; so, too, are a lock and key, and a battery-operated warning device.

See *Ambient Temperature, Chest Freezers, Upright Freezers* and *Fridge-freezers, Ventilation.*

## Size of Freezer

Generally allow between 2-5 cu ft (56l– 140l) per person when buying a freezer. The larger figure takes into account large-scale bulk-buying of meat, for instance, or quantities of home-produced vegetables or fruit. Your freezer will probably be divided roughly into thirds – meat, fruit and vegetables, and cooked dishes, though again bulk meat buys or produce-freezing may mean you have more of these than of cooked dishes.

## Smells

A smell of food that has gone off may be noticeable from a broken pack of over-blanched vegetables, or from a fatty food that has been stored for too long and has begun to go rancid. A more likely cause of smells in the freezer would be insufficient wrapping of pungent foods such as curries or garlic-flavoured dishes, onions, cheese or cauliflower. Smells can be dealt with when you defrost– wash the interior with 4tbs vinegar to 2pts (1l) warm water. Or you can buy an air purifier.

Avoid smells appearing by overwrapping the foods at risk, and open-freezing them inside a large bag.

See *Defrosting, Packaging.*

## Storage Capacity. See *Capacity.*

## Storage Times

Frozen foods will keep for ever, like the mammoth; but the dogs who were given frozen mammoth meat will have noticed that the flavour and texture were no longer perfect. To be sure that your food has these qualities intact, eat within the recommended storage times; but the food may still taste just as good after this time, and it will be perfectly safe to eat provided you have prepared and stored it properly.

See Basic Freezer Management.

## Syrup Pack

Light-coloured fruits, such as peaches, are liable to discolour easily, particularly on thawing. This is prevented by immersing the fruit in syrup so that it cannot come into contact with air. Make the syrup in advance so that it has had time to cool before the fruit is prepared. The syrup can be light or heavy, according to taste; 4oz (100g) of sugar to 1pt (500ml) of water makes a light syrup; 1½lb (600g) of sugar to 1pt (500ml) makes a very heavy one. Most people prefer a fairly light one: 8oz (200g) sugar to 1pt (500ml). Dissolve the sugar in the water and boil for 2 minutes to remove air bubbles. Cool and chill.

Fruit that discolours very easily, such as white cherries and apples, may benefit from the added fail-safe of extra vitamin C. Sprinkle lemon juice or ascorbic acid solution over the fruit or add ¼ tsp ascorbic acid to each pt (500 ml) of the syrup. Place the fruit in a rigid container and cover it with the syrup. Use crumpled cellophane or greaseproof to keep the fruit below the surface of the syrup as it freezes. Leave ½ in (1 cm) headspace and cover.

**Temperatures**

The temperature of the freezer normally should be 0°F (—18°C), and a freezer thermometer can be used to check this. For fast-freezing the temperature should be lower than this to freeze the food quickly, and to prevent other packs being warmed by the fresh food. The fast-freeze switch allows the temperature to drop to between —13° and —18°F (—25° and —28°C). All commercial freezing is done at lower temperatures than this, but it would be impractical and very expensive for a home freezer to go down to these.

**Thawing**

Some foods do not need to be thawed at all before being cooked. These are vegetables (with the exception of corn on the cob), unbaked pastry cases, convenience foods such as beefburgers and fish fingers. Small chops and fish fillets can also be cooked from frozen.

Fruit is best served still cold enough to have a few ice crystals in the cells so that it doesn't lose its shape. Thaw it in its container slowly in the fridge or at room temperature. If you are cooking the fruit, you can cook it from frozen as long as you heat it gently at first to stop it sticking. Sauces that have separated on thawing can be whisked to restore their texture.

See *Thawing*, and individual entries in the food section; also Cooking from Frozen, *Microwave Thawing, Separating, Salmonella*.

## Thermometer

You can buy a freezer thermometer (it doesn't cost much) to check that your freezer temperatures are correct (see above).

## Thermometer, Meat

This is essential when you are roasting from frozen. Don't try to use it while the meat is still frozen, but about 20 minutes before the meat should be ready you can plunge it right into the centre (avoiding the bone) and the temperature on the dial will tell you how near to being cooked the meat is.

## Thermostat

When you buy the freezer, the thermostat should be set to the correct temperatures (see temperatures above). You can make sure that the thermostat is operating correctly by using a freezer thermometer to check the temperature. If necessary, adjust the thermostat – and if there is anything seriously wrong, contact the manufacturer.

## Trays

You can buy special plastic freezer trays for open-freezing, or you can use non-stick baking dishes, plates or foil. Metal will not affect the food.

## Unblanched Vegetables

Brussels sprouts will keep for only 3 days in the freezer, but lima beans will keep for 3 weeks, corn on the cob and string beans for 4 weeks, and peas for as long as 6-9 months and small carrots for 12 months. So if you don't have time to blanch and will soon be eating the vegetables, you can risk storing some of them unblanched. For best colour and texture, though, it is best to blanch all vegetables.

## Unused Space

If your freezer is more empty than it should be, fill with boxes containing crumpled newspaper to cut down on running costs. Stack the boxes in the top section of an upright freezer.

## Upright Freezers

These are more expensive to buy and to run than chest freezers, and need defrosting more often. However they are often easier to find room for in the home, and they are more convenient to use, with the food easily accessible on the shelves, though large packs may be difficult to store. They use more electricity because opening the door allows a chilly stream of cold air to fall out, and over your feet, as cold air is heavier than warm air. The motor then has to work for a while to remove the warm air that will have replaced it. If food is clearly labelled and easy to find, the door will not have to be open long enough to allow too much cold air to escape. Models that have flaps across the fronts of the shelves keep the cold air inside, too. You will also find models with separate spring-hinged doors, and pull-out plastic baskets. The constant interchange of warm and cold air leads to the formation of frost and ice in the cabinet and therefore the necessity of more frequent defrosting: 3 or 4 times a year. Keep the frost down in between times with a plastic spatula. A few upright freezers have an automatic defrost (or 'frost-free') system which means they defrost themselves regularly; but they are expensive and cost more to run than the conventional models.

Upright freezers will fit more easily than chest types into the kitchen – but make sure they are not too close to the stove and that they have adequate ventilation. Most models have left or right opening doors. If the freezer is to go upstairs, remember that the stress on the floor will be high, because all the weight is concentrated in a small square.

New models have refrigerated shelves for fast freezing – otherwise foods to be frozen should be stacked against the bottom and sides.

A strong magnetic door seal is important – the door must be firmly closed to prevent warm air getting in. A drainage outlet that avoids having to mop up when defrosting is a useful extra.

See *Chest Freezers, Fast-freeze, Fridge-freezers, Loading, Siting*.

## Ventilation

A current of air around the freezer will prevent condensation – allow 2-4 in (5-10 cm). Models with a skin-type condenser will need space around for the heat to escape, and those with fan-assisted condensers need space at the grill outlet.

See *Ambient Temperature, Condenser*.

## Warning Light On

Check whether the door is open (may be due to a build-up of frost holding it slightly open), whether the thermostat is set high enough, whether the ambient temperature is too warm. It may be that you have put too much fresh food into the freezer, or that the fan unit or condenser grill needs to be freed from dust.

See *Ambient Temperature, Servicing, Thermostat*.

## Waxed Cartons

These containers, of the type that hold orange juice or milk, are being used less for the freezer now as polythene containers take over. The tall, square cartons with self-closing tops are useful for liquids and fruit, but are best lined with plastic. Don't allow the cartons to become heated, in case the wax melts.

See *Rigid Containers*.

# FREEZER MANAGEMENT

# Basic Freezer Management

Once you have your freezer you'll want to be sure you're using it to the best advantage. You will, of course, choose only top quality foods for freezing and package them correctly. This means excluding as much air as possible, carefully sealing, labelling and dating all packages. To earn its keep your freezer has to work for you. So right from the start, plan how it can do this.

Think back over your month's menus before you had a freezer. Are you, or do you want to be, a family that has a cooked main meal every day, or do you prefer snacks or individual tray meals, to suit a family whose members eat at different times? If the latter, then whenever you're baking cakes, pies, puddings, casseroles or stews, double or treble your quantities, eat one lot and freeze the rest in family or individual portions.

Do you have to prepare packed lunches? Then you'll want to make sandwiches, pâtés and pies in quantity.

If you've a young family you'll probably want a good supply of sausages, beefburgers, fish fingers, ice creams and mousses always at the ready.

If you're planning to bulk-buy do so wisely. Large packs of vegetables are invariably cheaper than the small ones. With meat, however, think carefully before investing in a whole carcass. Remember your package deal will include fat, bones and probably many cuts you'd never normally buy. Better to choose just the cuts you use and buy these in bulk, ready-frozen if you prefer, then keep an eye open for any special offers your butcher may have on such things as mince and stewing steak.

But don't get carried away in an attempt to fill your freezer. Ask yourself before you buy several barrels of the local farmer's bargain glut-crop apples (a) how much puréed/sliced/cooked apples your family will eat before next year's crop, and (b) how much freezer room you can spare.

Aim for a varied and steadily turned round stock. For the most economic use of your freezer it should be kept at least three-quarters full and stock should be turned round two or three times a year. It may not be practical with all items, but the chart below will give guidance on maximum recommended storage times.

*Vegetables*

Herbs - 6 months
Most vegetables - 12 months
Mushrooms: raw - 1 month
Mushrooms: cooked - 3 months
Onions - 3-6 months

*Fruit*

Fruit pies - 6 months
Purées - 12 months
Fruit: stoned - 12 months
Fruit: unstoned - 3 months
Soft fruit - 12 months

*Meat* (uncooked)

Beef - 8 months
Lamb - 6 months
Pork - 6 months
Mince, offal, tripe - 3 months
Sausages - 6 months
Bacon joints: smoked - 8 weeks
Bacon joints: unsmoked - 5 weeks
Bacon rashers and chops: smoked or unsmoked, vacuum-packed - 6 months

*Poultry & Game*

Chicken and fowls - 12 months
Ducks, game - 6 months
Giblets - 2 months

*Fish*

White fish - 3 months
Oily fish - 2 months

*Dairy Produce*

Eggs - 6 months
Butter: unsalted - 6 months
Butter: salted - 3 months
Cream (35% butterfat & over) - 3 months
Clotted cream - 12 months
Cream cheese - 6 weeks
Hard cheese - 3 months

*Bakery Produce*

Bread & rolls: crisp - 1 week
Bread: white and brown - 6 months
Sandwiches, scones - 2-6 months
Sponge cakes: undecorated - 4 months
Pastry: baked - 6 months
Pastry: unbaked - 3 months

The efficient management of a freezer which is kept well stocked is dependent on a record of contents. Try to keep a freezer book and use it every time you put something in or take something out. Then you won't waste hours searching for an item that no longer exists.

Suggested headings could be as below.

| Food | Package size | No. of packages | Date of freezing | Taken out |
|------|------|------|------|------|
| **Runner Beans** | **1lb (500g) bags** | **8** | **30th July, 1979** | **1** |

Work out an easy colour code. If your favourite freezer centre uses a colour code as part of its sign-posting, copy their code. Generally blue is used for fish, red for meat, orange or yellow for fruit, green for vegetables.

Keep foods of a kind together. A big blue plastic sack or

nylon shopping bag to hold all fish packs, a green one for vegetables and so on. Then when you want to find that last pack of runner beans all you have to do is haul out the green bag and rummage through that. The specially designed baskets are ideal for dividing a chest freezer into compartments, but cardboard boxes from the grocer will do. Fit the boxes with string handles so they can be lifted out easily; use coloured twine for identification.

Having worked out a plan that suits you and put it into action, the only other chore will be an occasional defrosting. Some freezers are self-defrosting but if you have to do the job yourself choose a time when stocks are low, then proceed as follows.

Switch off. Remove food, pack it into cardboard boxes (if it isn't already in them), cover with a blanket. Put towels or a piece of plastic foam at the bottom of the freezer and scrape the frost off the sides. Remove foam or towels carefully taking all the bits of frost with them. Wipe over the inside of the freezer with a solution of 1 tbs bicarbonate of soda to 1 quart (1 l) warm water. Wipe dry with a clean cloth and switch on again. Leave the freezer running about an hour then replace the food.

Finally, you may not want your freezer serviced regularly, but find out if there's a good maintenance engineer on 24-hour call in your district - before you need him - and keep a note of his telephone number by the freezer.

# Correct Freezer Loading

Loading an upright freezer is a fairly simple job because it's already divided into compartments with either baskets or shelves. So it's just a question of deciding which section to use for which types of food.

Loading a chest freezer is not quite so simple if you want some semblance of order.

For all freezers it's a good idea to have a chart attached to the outside showing where the different foods are: which layer or shelf, which colour box or bag, so no one has to go scrabbling through, wrecking your carefully devised system of packing.

Whenever possible, shape bag packs into neat squares or oblongs - awkward shapes take up more room and are difficult to stack. A good way to do this is to stand polythene bags in empty freezer cartons, pour in your soup, fruit purée or whatever. Stand them on a tray in the freezer until hard then remove bags from the cartons, seal, label and return to the freezer.

Label all packs - you won't be able to identify them even a week later - on the side for upright freezers and on the top for chest freezers.

With an upright freezer you might find it easier for loading, as well as using, if you divide catering packs of fruits and vegetables into smaller units. And put economy meat packs, in family or individual portions, into polythene bags. Seal them, label and stack as carefully as possible to avoid wasting space. Don't forget when re-packing to put the date on each of the labels.

Items for long-term storage should go in the lower part of the freezer, the least accessible part. Pack them neatly and closely, but not so close together that you can't get your fingers between them to manoeuvre them out. Door shelves are useful for smaller items and those with a short storage life such as butter, pâtés, packs of home-made soup and sauces, one-portion packs or left-overs.

With a chest freezer you'll find life easier if you divide it into compartments. Do this by means of wire baskets, cardboard boxes, coloured nylon shopping bags or large coloured polythene bags. You then keep each category of food in one section.

The bottom layer you will use for bulky and long-term storage items. Above this will come the items you'll be using in the next month or so: supplies of fruit and vegetables, bread and cakes, meat and cooked dishes. The top layer will be for quick turnover items such as sandwiches, soups, sauces, ice creams, puddings, plate meals, left-overs and for smaller items - packs of herbs, breadcrumbs, grated cheese, stock cubes etc. - that are apt to get lost or forgotten if allowed to slip to the bottom. Try to keep the fast-freezing section fairly free so that it's ready for freezing fresh foods without a lot of upheaval.

These sketches of an upright and chest freezer give you some idea how a plan-packed freezer should look.

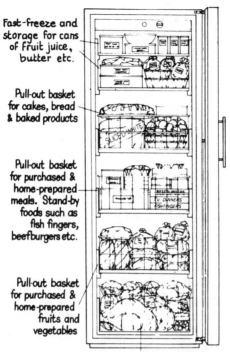

Fast-freeze and storage for cans of fruit juice, butter etc.

Pull-out basket for cakes, bread & baked products

Pull-out basket for purchased & home-prepared meals. Stand-by foods such as fish fingers, beefburgers etc.

Pull-out basket for purchased & home-prepared fruits and vegetables

Pull-out basket for large, bulky packages of meat, poultry etc.

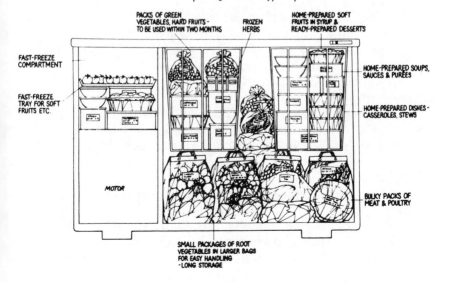

PACKS OF GREEN VEGETABLES, HARD FRUITS - TO BE USED WITHIN TWO MONTHS

FROZEN HERBS

HOME-PREPARED SOFT FRUITS IN SYRUP & READY-PREPARED DESSERTS

FAST-FREEZE COMPARTMENT

FAST-FREEZE TRAY FOR SOFT FRUITS ETC.

HOME-PREPARED SOUPS, SAUCES & PURÉES

HOME-PREPARED DISHES - CASSEROLES, STEWS

MOTOR

BULKY PACKS OF MEAT & POULTRY

SMALL PACKAGES OF ROOT VEGETABLES IN LARGER BAGS FOR EASY HANDLING - LONG STORAGE

# Blanching Vegetables

Blanching is another word for scalding, just a quick immersion in boiling water. It's not, as some people think, to kill bugs or tenderise vegetables.

If you freeze your garden vegetables unblanched you're not likely to be running health risks. If there are any bugs in the vegetables they would either be removed in washing, or else become entirely inactive when frozen and be destroyed when you cooked the vegetables.

So why bother to blanch? Because there's a group of chemical substances called enzymes that go on working even under your freezer's sub-zero conditions.

Enzymes won't poison you. In fact there are similar ones in the human digestive system. Their job is to break down food. But if they're not scalded they will, in time, affect the colour and flavour of vegetables.

You should have all the equipment needed already in your kitchen:

Pan to hold 6-8 pts (3-4 l) boiling water.

Immersing container to hold the vegetables. Could be a wire basket of the chip-pan variety, a bigger collapsible one, a muslin bag or nylon wine-straining bag.

Cooking timer – the 'pinger', or a stop-watch that works to the minute.

Really cold water, a plentiful supply running from the tap or lots of ice cubes and a big basin of cold water.

Colander or sieve for quick draining of vegetables after cooking.

Chart of blanching times.

When you have assembled your equipment, proceed like this:

Bring water to the boil. When at a good fast boil, use wire basket or fabric bag to lower just 1 lb (500 g) of vegetables into the water. Start timing from the minute the water has

176

come back to the boil. (That's why you do only this amount at a time – the water stays on the boil more easily, and vegetables can move about enough to let the water really penetrate.)

Watch your timing like a hawk. If when blanching cauliflower florets you give them one minute over the recommended three, the result is mushy cauliflower.

The same goes for cooling. Whether you use cold tap water or a bowl of ice-cold water (keep on adding more cubes as it warms up) you need to cool scalded vegetables for the same length of time as given for blanching. If you don't cool properly, the cooking process that you started will just go on inside again giving mushy results.

Then drain. Tip from wire basket or fabric bag into a colander. When vegetables stop dripping, spread on shallow trays and put into the freezer (to open-freeze until solid enough to pack in big polythene bags, giving a free-flow pack). Or put into bags or plastic containers in single-meal size servings.

You can do 6-7 consecutive batches of vegetables in the same water (bringing it back to the boil each time, of course) and this helps to retain the vitamin C content. Another advantage of blanching is that it has been proved that once your frozen vegetables are cooked there's more vitamin C retained in the ones that have been blanched than in those that have not.

## Preparation, Blanching and Cooling of Vegetables

(Note: if vegetables are very young, very freshly picked they may need very slightly less blanching time than recommended below. Experiment with crops labelled with how long you blanched them if you want to perfect your technique.)

| Vegetable | Preparation | Blanching and Cooling Time (same for both) |
|---|---|---|
| Asparagus | Choose stems all same thickness. Cut length to fit container. Do not tie in bunches. | Thick stalks - 2 minutes. Medium stalks - 3 minutes. Thick stalks - 4 minutes. |
| Beans (Lima) | Choose small, young beans. Pod. | 2 minutes. |
| Beans (String) | Either slice fairly thickly or (better for flavour) cut into 1-in (2-cm) chunks. | Chunky cut or whole - 2 minutes. Sliced - 1 minute. |
| Broccoli | Trim to even lengths with compact heads and cut off any tough stalks. | Thin stalks - 3 minutes. Thicker - 4 minutes. |
| Brussels Sprouts | Trim off outer leaves to achieve small, tight sprouts evenly sized. | 3 minutes. |
| Carrots | Leave small, young carrots whole, slice or dice larger ones. | Small or whole - 5 minutes. Diced or sliced - 3 minutes. |
| Cauliflower | Separate into small sprigs ('florets'). Wash well. | 3 minutes. |
| Celeriac | Wash, trim, scrape. Cut into large dice. | 4 minutes. |
| Corn on the Cob | Remove husks and silk. Trim stems. | 4 to 8 minutes according to size. |

| Eggplant | Wash, cut into ½-in (1-cm) slices. | 4 minutes. |
|---|---|---|
| Leeks | Remove outer leaves. Trim ends. Wash well. | 2 to 4 minutes according to size. |
| Mushrooms | Wash and dry well. If cultivated, need not be peeled. | Do not blanch in water - instead sauté in butter, drain, cool, then freeze. |
| Onion | Peel, slice or chop (if wanted for later use in made-up dishes). | 2 minutes. |
| Parsnips | Choose small young ones. Scrape, wash, slice or dice. | 2 minutes. |
| Peas | Only very young tender ones should be used. Sort carefully. | 1 minute. |
| Rutabagas | Remove thick peel, cut into cubes. | 3 minutes. |
| Spinach | Use young tender leaves or carefully remove tough mid-rib of older leaves. Wash well. | 2 minutes. |
| Turnips | Remove thick peel, cut into cubes. | 2 minutes. |
| Zucchini | Cut into 1-in (2-cm) slices. | 1 minute. |

# The Fast-freeze Switch

Whether it's known as fast-freeze or auto-freeze or super-cold or extra-freeze - or whatever a bright manufacturer's adman can think up - it's a control with a very definite purpose.

The way food freezes affects its final quality. Most of us know that watery foods, like cucumbers and strawberries, are mushier after freezing than when fresh. They can be used in cooked dishes, but once thawed fully, they are not exactly crisp. This is because the water content inside forms ice crystals. It happens in all foods, but obviously the more water the more crystals. And these crystals break up the internal cell structure of the food. Slow freezing allows these crystals to build up. The faster the freezing the smaller the crystals.

The big commercial companies that freeze meat for shipping, for instance, do it at much, much lower temperatures than our ordinary domestic freezers could achieve. That's why you should notice little if any difference between commercially frozen-then-thawed meat and fresh-killed. At the truly deep-freeze temperatures of commercial freezing, few if any ice crystals have the chance to form.

So we fast-freeze to keep the food's structure as perfect as possible. But there is another reason, too. All fresh food, even if it feels cold to the touch, has a kind of body heat of its own. We call it 'fresh-warm'. When you introduce fresh-warm food to the freezer, its body heat has the effect of raising the temperature in there. And too much fresh warmth could affect the condition of the rest of the frozen food in storage. If the temperature of your already-frozen food begins to rise, that begins to form ice crystals and we're back to square one.

So how does your fast-freeze switch try to counteract all this?

The parts of the freezer that need concern us here are the motor and the thermostat. The motor keeps the freezer just as cold as the thermostat tells it to. The motor switches itself on and off as often as necessary to keep the overall inside temperature down to the accepted storage level of $0°F$ ($-18°C$) or less. When you use the fast-freeze control you are making the motor ignore the thermostat and (just like a central heating system in reverse) it keeps the freezer temperature dropping, dropping, to at least $-18°F$ ($-28°C$) and often lower, depending on the make of freezer, its size, and how full it is.

The instruction book that comes with your freezer should tell you the temperature range of the model. If it doesn't, you can check by buying a freezer thermometer. Switch the freezer to normal for 24 hours then take a reading; switch to fast-freeze for 3 hours then take another reading.

Look at your instruction book to see how much fresh-warm food you can fast-freeze within any 24 hours. If it doesn't tell you, or if you haven't the book, you can generally assume that you can fast-freeze one-tenth of the freezer's capacity: e.g. a 12 cu ft (339 l) freezer, capacity 240 lb, (120 kg), will freeze down 24 lb (12 kg) of fresh food in 24 hours.

Some freezers have a separate fast-freeze compartment of a size that tells you how much fresh food can go in there without affecting the temperature of food elsewhere in the cabinet. Others have no separate compartment; but when the fast-freeze switch is on the temperature of the whole inside of the cabinet is lowered.

If there is no separate fast-freeze compartment it makes sense to put your fresh-warm food in the coldest part of the freezer and move other packages away if possible. In a chest freezer stack fresh-warm goods against the walls. In an upright, try to keep all fresh-warm food on one shelf either at top or bottom, and against the walls unless your freezer has freezing coils within the shelves.

*Using the fast-freeze switch.* This is where it pays to

think ahead. Before you put in your fresh-warm food, switch on the fast-freeze control for 2-3 hours, or until a thermometer check gives you a reading of —18° F (—28° C) or lower.

Keep it on for 24 hours at the most after introducing the food – more than that might cause the motor to overheat, and in any case is wasteful of electricity. If your freezer is reasonably full, and not kept in a very warm room, it will then take another 8 to 10 hours for the thermostat to bring the temperature back up to the usual storage level. And it's a good idea to give the fast-freeze a day's rest after this, disturbing the food as little as possible.

*Must you fast-freeze?* Even when you're just putting in a little bit of left-over gravy or a pound of meat? No, providing you've cooled the food beforehand to ordinary coldness, you can freeze 2 lb (1 kg) or so quickly enough at ordinary storage temperature, especially if you remember to move other packages away and to put fresh food near the freezer wall.

And now the hard question. How long is long enough, when you are fast-freezing a quantity of foods? So much depends on make of freezer, kind of food, size of freezer and how much is already stored – it's almost impossible to give a firm rule. The following is a rough guide.

| | |
|---|---|
| Bacon, meat, poultry | 2 hours per lb (500 g) |
| Fish | 2 hours per lb (500 g) |
| Vegetables and fruit | 1 hour per lb (500 g) |
| Prepared meals | 2 hours per lb (500 g) |
| Bread and cakes | 1 hour per lb (500 g) |
| Pastries | 2 hours per lb (500 g) |
| Dairy products | 1 hour per lb (500 g) |
| Liquids | 1 hour per lb (500 g) |

# Thawing and Re-freezing

## Thawing

A quick rule of thumb for judging how long food should be thawed is generally: overnight in the fridge. So on Saturday night you'd get out the joint you want to roast for Sunday lunch. When it's in the fridge the food will be thawing slowly but safely.

There are, of course, several exceptions to this rule. Frozen vegetables are much nicer if cooked from frozen, counting the cooking time from the moment the water comes back to the boil. Anyone who's bought a pack of commercially frozen peas hardly needs to be told that!

In fact, the makers of frozen foods usually meet a sort of thawing-in-reverse question. People worry about whether it will be all right if frozen vegetables have accidentally been allowed to thaw before cooking. The answer is that from the point of view of health there is no problem - unless of course the packet has been thawing for days, in which case your nose will tell you in the usual way. But commercially frozen vegetables have been picked at the very peak of their freshness, handled carefully, blanched swiftly and frozen speedily - so it is not surprising that manufacturers wince at the thought of all that effort being wasted if vegetables are allowed to soften and 'age' a bit during a thawing process that isn't necessary.

You can generally take it that any pre-packed food that carries 'COOK FROM FROZEN' instructions has been marked that way for reasons of appetite appeal, not just for safety. The food has been tested and found to cook better, taste nicer, if cooked from the frozen state.

So what are the foods you must thaw? The most important is raw poultry. Because there is a health risk, complicated to explain but proven, if your oven heat doesn't penetrate right to the middle of the bones of a bird, where dormant microbes can lurk.

But although we must thaw poultry it is perfectly alright to cook meat from frozen. There is not the same kind of health risk if meat is on the bone. In fact, it is really only essential to pre-thaw meat if it has been boned and rolled. There's just a chance that some micro-organisms might have been transferred to the inside of the meat during the boning and rolling process. Otherwise, meat on or off the bone can be cooked from frozen or not, as you please.

Experiment for yourself. If you have the kind of household that's likely to want an impromptu roast you'll probably want to cook it from frozen. If you don't thaw overnight, it must be admitted that waiting for a thawing joint to be ready can be maddeningly like watching the pot that never boils. A 3 lb (1½ kg) piece of beef, for instance, takes about six hours to thaw completely in a room temperature of around 70°F (21°C). And it's not wise to have a piece of meat sitting around for that length of time at that temperature.

Fruit is a food that can be made or marred by the thawing. The soft berry fruits are nicest if they still have a cold edge to them when eaten - 2 hours at room temperature is ample thawing time for a pint (500 ml) of berries still in their container. If you happen to let them over-thaw, pop them back into the freezer for a few moments to re-chill before serving. Other fruits, the kinds with tougher skins like apricots and peaches and cherries, need no more than 4 hours' thawing - the same for apple slices or rhubarb. It is a good idea, too, to turn the sealed container over once or twice during the thawing time, to move the fruit about and make sure that the thawing is taking place evenly.

Finally there is a way to speed up the thawing process when you're in a real hurry. Here are a few tips.

With meat or poultry, it helps to put it, still wrapped and sealed, in a sinkful of lukewarm water. The cold of the parcel will quickly chill the water, which you may need to change after about ten minutes. Don't be tempted to use really hot water - the thawing would be too rapid and uneven.

With bread, of course, you can take slices and toast them from frozen, or wrap an unsliced loaf in foil and warm gently in the oven. Once thawed in the oven, however, the bread goes stale more quickly, so if possible slice off what you need and return the rest to the freezer.

## Thawing Timetable (Times given are approximate)

| | In refrigerator | At room temperature |
|---|---|---|
| Cream | 8 hours per ¼ pint (150 ml) | 1-2 hours |
| Cheese | 8 hours per ½ lb (250 g) | 2 hours |
| Butter | 4 hours per ½ lb (250 g) | 1-2 hours |
| Meat - Beef, Lamb, Veal, Pork | 5 hours per lb (500 g) 5 hours per lb (500 g) | 2 hours per lb (500 g) Thaw in fridge only |
| Chops, Steaks, Sausages | 6 hours per lb (500 g) | 2 hours per lb (500 g) |
| Minced Meat | 10-12 hours per lb (500g) | 2 hours per lb (500 g) |
| Offal - Kidney, Liver | 8-9 hours per lb (500g) | 1-1½ hours per lb (500 g) |
| Chicken | Under 4 lb (2 kg) - 12 hours 4 lb (2 kg) and over - 1-1½ days | Thaw in fridge only |
| Fruits | 8-10 hours in container | 2-4 hours in container |

## Power Cuts

The threat of power cuts can dismay and worry new freezer owners. In fact power cuts are rarely disastrous as they don't often last more than a couple of hours, and providing a few simple rules are followed, food is perfectly safe in the freezer for up to 24 hours.

If you have advance warning of a power cut, here's what to do.

Move ice cream and cream cakes (if in rigid container) to bottom or back of freezer and stack more dense items, such as meat, on the top or at the front.

Fill any gaps with boxes or newspaper to cut down the air circulation.

Switch on to fast-freeze for a couple of hours.

Don't open the door or lid until power is back and the freezer has had time to get back to normal temperature.

## Re-freezing

But what if you do have an extended cut, breakdown, or power is accidentally switched off and the food thaws? Can you re-freeze it?

There's no simple answer: some foods you can re-freeze, some you can't.

First, the food must still be fresh. If it has gone off throw it out. Don't take risks. The freezer can't make food fresher or kill bacteria. Food comes out of the freezer in the same condition as when it went in.

When food is thawed and re-frozen, the cell structure can be damaged, which means there may be a loss of colour, texture, flavour and nutritional value.

So providing the thawed food was hygienically packed, here's a guide to what you can salvage.

*Fruit:* because of its high water content, fruit collapses, so don't re-freeze in the same form. Instead use it to make purées or syrups.

*Vegetables:* best re-frozen only if cooked thoroughly and used in dishes, stews, soups and purées. Vegetable purée is a useful addition to many dishes for extra flavour and thickening.

*Raw meat, fish and poultry:* never re-freeze these. Instead, cook first and make into casseroles, pies, roasts or stews. Turn fish into flans, fish-cakes, casseroles.

*Prepared meals:* cooked meat or fish dishes should not be re-frozen.

*Bread, cakes, pastry:* can be re-frozen, except for cakes containing cream. Bread will be a little staler.

186

*Ice cream, cream and synthetic cream:* never re-freeze these, or any foods containing them.

All this can only be a guide. It must be up to the individual to use his or her commonsense - and nose - to decide whether to re-freeze thawed food. Only you will know how hygienically your food was packed and stored, how soft it has become, how long it has already been in the freezer.

But, once food has been re-frozen, it should be used up as soon as possible.

# Cooking from Frozen

Most foods can be cooked from frozen, and prepared items like fish fingers, beefburgers, raw pastry, patties and vegetables are best cooked this way. It won't matter desperately, from health or nutrition points of view, if frozen foods accidentally thaw out for a short time before being cooked, but they may lose some of the fresh taste and texture that were locked in during the freezing.

Whole chickens, however, must be thoroughly thawed before cooking - if your oven heat doesn't penetrate right to the bone of a fowl, there's a risk that germs lurking there could cause food poisoning; and a frozen whole chicken won't cook from frozen without scorching on the outside before those parts near the bone are fully thawed.

As far as meat is concerned it's really a personal thing - you can cook a joint from frozen or thaw it overnight in the fridge. By cooking from frozen you'll have extra fuel cost and the bother of all that prodding with the thermometer. But there are many families where it's necessary to cook a joint from frozen at short notice, sometimes because there isn't enough spare fridge-space to let a joint thaw there overnight, for instance.

If you are cooking from frozen, this is the best way to keep the meat nice and juicy and avoid too much fuss.

A meat thermometer is essential for best results. They can be bought at most freezer centres and hardware departments of large stores. And a roasting bag or some foil prevents drying-out - especially useful for smaller joints as well as avoiding the need to clean the oven.

First calculate your cooking time according to how you like your meat. It should work out approximately as in the chart below but will vary a bit according to your individual oven and size of joint, and (see note later) on whether you are baking other things in the oven.

## Calculating your cooking time from frozen

| Beef | At 350°F, 180°C, about 55 mins to the lb (550g) for well-done beef; 50 mins to the lb (500g) for rare beef. |
|------|----------------------------------------------------------------------------------------------------------|
| Lamb | At 350°F, 180°C, about 60 mins to the lb (500g). |
| Pork | At 400°F, 200°C, about 60 mins to the lb (500g). |

These times do NOT mean that you need to pre-heat the oven. It's best to work out timing beforehand, then put the meat in, set the oven and start roasting from cold.

How you put the meat in depends on whether you use a roasting bag or foil. If a bag, snip a small slit in the upper side, loosely twist-tie it, allowing room for the juices to self-baste the meat. If foil, and unless you want rare beef, put an inch of water plus a stock cube in the bottom of the smallest roasting pan that your joint will fit in, then cover with foil.

About 20 minutes before your calculated end of cooking time, plunge your meat thermometer into the centre of the meat. If the meat has a bone, you have to try to get as near as possible to the bone without touching it. (This is a good argument for using a transparent roasting bag, because you can plunge the thermometer through the slit; otherwise you must, of course, fold back foil to see what you're at.) Look for these temperature readings:

| Beef | 170° F (77° C) - well done |
|------|----------------------------|
|      | 160° F (71° C) - medium done |
|      | 150° F (66° C) - rare |
|      | 140° F (60° C) - very rare (best served cold) |
| Lamb | 180° F (82° C) - well done |
|      | 170° F (77° C) - pinkish |
| Pork | 190° F (88° C) - well done |
|      | (pork should never be undercooked) |

By checking with the thermometer at this stage you should, with a bit of practice, be able to calculate how much longer to go on roasting before reaching the required stage. And if you want a crisper outside to the meat – e.g. crackling on pork – now's the time to cut the roasting bag and fold it back, or remove foil.

Smaller cuts of meat can, of course, always be cooked from frozen in a hurry. Steaks and chops can be grilled by placing them 2 in (5 cm) further away from the heat than usual. When almost cooked place nearer the heat to brown.

If frying, again start at a lower heat than usual and raise the temperature for the last few minutes to brown. Expect grilling or frying to take 5-10 minutes longer than cooking from thawed.

The factors that can affect your timing show how approximate any timing charts must be. If, for instance, you introduce a frozen pie to the oven, it will have the effect of lowering the baking temperature for a while. Or you may live in an area where, on busy Sunday roasting mornings, local power supplies can fluctuate. It is a matter of trial and error, but there will be no harm done if you keep an eye on the meat thermometer.

If you want to roast potatoes, the longer, cooler cooking time involved in roasting frozen meat means allowing extra roasting time for the potatoes, so put them in earlier than usual in a separate dish with less fat than usual.

And talking of busy roasting Sundays, there is a restaurant technique that can come in handy if you get in a dither about serving frozen vegetables plus roast meat – you know, when the vegetables are either overcooking while you carve or else getting cold. The trade calls the process 'the refreshing of vegetables' and it's a trick that works well with peas, and chunky cut beans. Any time during your roasting morning just cook the frozen peas or beans for one minute less than the time recommended on the pack. Then take them out, put in a colander under the cold tap to cool gently but quickly, then cover with cold water. This holds the colour. At serving-up time, have a pan of briskly boiling, salted water on the hob, drain the cold vegetables and drop them in to boil for just one minute before serving. They'll be piping hot and will taste – and look – as if freshly cooked.

# Table of Equivalents

This table of approximate equivalents is based on convenient quantities rather than strictly accurate conversions.

## Temperature

| °F | °C |
|----|----|
| 225 | 110 |
| 250 | 130 |
| 275 | 140 |
| 300 | 150 |
| 325 | 170 |
| 350 | 180 |

| °F | °C |
|----|----|
| 375 | 190 |
| 400 | 200 |
| 425 | 220 |
| 450 | 230 |
| 475 | 240 |

## Weight

| Imp | Metric |
|-----|--------|
| ½ oz | 15 g |
| 1 oz | 25 g |
| 2 oz | 50 g |
| 3 oz | 75 g |
| 4 oz | 100-125 g |
| 5 oz | 150 g |
| 6 oz | 175 g |
| 7 oz | 200 g |
| 8 oz | 250 g |
| 9 oz | 275 g |
| 10 oz | 300 g |
| 11 oz | 325 g |

| Imp | Metric |
|-----|--------|
| 12 oz | 350 g |
| 13 oz | 375 g |
| 14 oz | 400 g |
| 15 oz | 450 g |
| 1 lb | 500 g |
| 1½ lb | 750 g |
| 2 lb | 1 kg |
| 3 lb | 1.5 kg |
| 3½ lb | 1.75 kg |
| 4 lb | 2 kg |
| 5 lb | 2.5 kg |

## Liquid

| Imp | Metric | Imp | Metric |
| --- | --- | --- | --- |
| ¼ pt | 150 ml | 2½ pt | 1.5 l |
| ½ pt | 300 ml | 3 pt | 1.75 l |
| ¾ pt | 450 ml | 4 pt | 2.25 l |
| 1 pt | 600 ml | 5 pt | 3 l |
| 1½ pt | 900 ml | 6 pt | 3.5 l |
| 1¾ pt | 1 litre (l) | 7 pt | 4.0 l |
| 2 pt | 1.25 l | 8 pt | 4.5 l |

## Spoons (level)

| Imp | Metric | Imp | Metric |
| --- | --- | --- | --- |
| ¼ tsp | 1.25 ml | 1 tsp | 5 ml |
| ½ tsp | 2.5 ml | 1 tbs | 15 ml |

## Length

| Imp | Metric | Imp | Metric |
| --- | --- | --- | --- |
| ¼″ | 5 mm | 8″ | 20.0 cm |
| ½″ | 1.0 cm | 9″ | 23.0 cm |
| 1″ | 2.5 cm | 10″ | 25.0 cm |
| 2″ | 5.0 cm | 12″ | 30.0 cm |
| 3″ | 7.5 cm | 15″ | 38.0 cm |
| 4″ | 10.0 cm | 18″ | 45.0 cm |
| 5″ | 12.5 cm | 24″ | 60.0 cm |
| 6″ | 15.0 cm | 36″ | 92.0 cm |
| 7″ | 17.5 cm | | |